FOREWORD BY JEFF HOFFMAN

The MIRACLE MORNING

for COLLEGE STUDENTS

The Not-So-Obvious Secrets to Success in College and Life

Hal Elrod • Natalie Janji

With Honorée Corder

THE MIRACLE MORNING FOR COLLEGE STUDENTS

Hal Elrod & Natalie Janji
with Honorée Corder

Interior Design: Christina Culbertson, 3CsBooks.com

Paperback ISBN- 978-1-942589-17-4

Digital IBSN- 978-1-942589-18-1

DEDICATIONS

Hal

This book is dedicated to the people who mean more to me than anything in the world—my family. Mom, Dad, my sister, Hayley, my wife, Ursula, and our two children—Sophie and Halsten. I love you all more than I can put into words!

This book is also in loving memory of my sister, Amery Kristine Elrod.

Natalie

This book is dedicated to my family. To my ancestors that made this all possible, thank you. Mom, Dad, and George, you were there for me through the ups and downs, and I am forever grateful. Mom, thank you for your constant love, vibrant energy, and support of my dreams. Dad, thank you for all your hard work over the years and showing me the power in a smile. George, thank you for being the greatest brother, best friend, and supporter I could have ever wished for.

Thank you for everything.

I love you all so much!

CONTENTS

SECTION I: The Miracle Morning + Life S.A.V.E.R.S.

The case for mornings and why they are critically important to a college student's success (and what happens when you don't take advantage of them).

Even if you've never been a morning person, you're about to discover the simplest and most effective way to overcome the challenge of waking up early, beat the snooze button, and maximize your mornings.

Harness the life-changing power of the most effective, proven personal development practices known to man, which are guaranteed to save you from missing out on the levels of success (in every area of your life) that you truly want and deserve.

SECTION II: The Not-So-Obvious College Student Success Principles

Discover why who you're becoming is significantly more important than what you say and do each day and precisely how to lead yourself to the next level so that you can take your success to the next level (because it only happens in that order).

When it comes to being a college student, managing your energy is significantly more important than managing your time. Discover how to strategically engineer your life to sustain extraordinary levels of physical, mental, and emotional energy.

Discover how to increase your academic productivity and get more done by developing your ability to consistently prioritize, plan, and maintain unwavering focus on your highest priorities, regardless of outside forces and distractions.

SECTION III: Level 10 College Student Success Skills

A SPECIAL INVITATION FROM HAL

R eaders and practitioners of *The Miracle Morning* have co-created an extraordinary community consisting of over 200,000 like-minded individuals from around the world who wake up each day with purpose and dedicate time to fulfilling the unlimited potential that is within all of us, while helping others to do the same.

As author of *The Miracle Morning*, I felt I had a responsibility to create an online community where readers could come together to connect, get encouragement, share best practices, support one another, discuss the book, post videos, find accountability partners, and even swap smoothie recipes and exercise routines.

However, I honestly had no idea that The Miracle Morning Community would become one of the most positive, engaged, and supportive online communities in the world—but it has. I'm constantly astounded by the caliber and character of our membership, which presently includes people from over 70 countries and is growing daily.

Just go to **www.MyTMMCommunity.com** and request to join The Miracle Morning Community on Facebook®. You'll immediately be able to connect with 80,000+ people who are already practicing TMM. While you'll find many who are just beginning their Miracle Morning journey, you'll discover even more who have been at it for years and who will happily share advice and guidance to accelerate your success.

I'll be moderating the Community and checking in regularly, so I look forward to seeing you there! If you'd like to reach out to me personally on social media, follow **@HalElrod** on Twitter and **Facebook.com/YoPalHal** on Facebook. Let's connect soon!

FOREWORD

by JEFF HOFFMAN
Co-founder of Priceline.com; Co-founder of ColorJar

Unless you're chasing your dreams,
you're just going through the motions.

A s a child, I lived in a small town in Arizona where no one ever left, and no one around me had big dreams. But I did. I dreamed of far-off places, exotic lands, exploring new cultures. I dreamed of seeing the world. And my dream was further fueled when I read this famous Mark Twain quote: *"Travel is fatal to prejudice, bigotry, and narrow-mindedness, and many of our people need it sorely on these accounts. Broad, wholesome, charitable views of men and things cannot be acquired by vegetating in one little corner of the earth all one's lifetime."*

Even as a child, I knew I wanted to see the world, and I believed I would. I just needed to figure out how. I had an idea, though—one that soon became my mantra. *Dream Big, Work Hard, Create Value.* I already had the dream. Now I needed to figure out where to focus my hard work and how to create value.

During high school, I decided that I wanted to go to a top college to get the education I needed to chase my dream. I wanted to go to Yale University. When I told people that I applied to Yale, they told me, "Jeff, how would someone like *you* get into a school like *Yale?*" To their disappointment, I was admitted into Yale, and I quickly left that small town that no one ever left. Yale was my dream school, and I was on my way.

Unfortunately, that dream slammed into a brick wall the first week of classes. I was told by the finance office that I couldn't stay at Yale because I didn't have enough money. I stood in that office and defiantly told everyone that I was not leaving until I had that diploma in my hands. But I didn't know how I was going to do it. I kept thinking: *What if I don't find the money to pay for Yale?* Feeling hopeless, I called my friends back home and asked them what I should do. They all told me to forget about Yale and come home. I realized right then that would have been the *worst* choice I could make. I thought: *What am I going to think of myself if I quit the first time I face an obstacle in my life?* Without missing a beat, I started my first company the following Friday. I paid my way through college and got my degree from Yale. Dreamers 1, Quitters 0. A good final score.

After graduating, I followed my parents' advice (and everyone else's) and got a job at a big company. But my dream was still alive. I taped a note card on my bathroom mirror with my biggest dream written on it: "Travel to 50 Countries." I looked at that note card every day as I got ready for work, with hopes that I was taking steps to get closer to that dream. One day at work, I ran into a friend in the elevator. In our conversation, we found out that both of us had been working at the same company for 3 years and had not run into each other. I worked on the fourth floor and he worked on the sixth floor. That's why our paths never crossed. Like a slap in my face, it hit me: *How am I going to accomplish my dream of travelling to 50 countries if I don't even visit the sixth floor?!* When I came home that day and looked at that note card taped to my bathroom mirror, I realized that I had not gotten any closer to accomplishing my dream. So, I left my secure corporate job. People thought I was crazy and irresponsible to do that, but I knew what I wanted, and I was going to work hard to make it a reality.

Since then, I have built and sold my own companies, been a CEO of public companies, been part of the founding team of a $60 billion company, produced movies in Hollywood, produced a Grammy-winning jazz album, and more. Oh, and I have visited almost 100 countries now. Dreams really do come true.

Why? Because I dreamed big, worked hard, and created value.

I first met Natalie at an Appreciative Inquiry summit for the non-profit charity 1Life Fully Lived, and was immediately inspired by her passion to help students. When I asked Natalie what her dreams were, she told me that her dream was to give college students the opportunity to dream their own dreams. She wants students to succeed far beyond what they could imagine. She is the unique expert for helping college students. With a heart of service, she wrote this book for *you*. I was once in your shoes, only I didn't have Natalie and this book to shine a light and guide my way. Luckily, you do.

When Natalie started college at Loyola Marymount University, she was undecided about what she wanted to do, but believed in her passion for helping others. She studied chemistry, but did not do well academically and remained unfulfilled as a student. She struggled with depression and anxiety, but never gave up hope for a better life. After reading *The Miracle Morning*, she realized she could create a future filled with purpose and joy. Through her journey from being a student "just getting by" to thriving in every area of her life, she realized she wanted to help other students overcome their own adversity to be their best. She gained clarity about her love of writing, and took a sharp turn from a potential career in chemistry to a career in helping others through her writing. I greatly admire Natalie's commitment to helping as many students as she can.

While watching her peers choose traditional paths after college, Natalie took a leap and decided she wanted to write a book about her college experience. She did not want to write just *any* book; she wanted to write a book in the *Miracle Morning* book series. Ever since she read *The Miracle Morning,* her dream was to write a book for college students with Hal. She believed that a Miracle Morning book for college students should exist, whether or not she was chosen to be the author of it. Natalie not only made the case for this book to become a reality, but also became the coauthor with Hal. Natalie *dreamed big, worked hard, and created value.*

This book will impact hundreds of thousands of students all around the world. *The Miracle Morning for College Students* is a guide for you to improve as a student, but more importantly as an individual. By practicing the *Life S.A.V.E.R.S.* and applying the wisdom that Natalie has delivered in the book, you will become the person ready to accomplish your dreams during your time in college. Page by page, you will begin your journey to a better you.

My wisdom for you is to *Dream Big, Work Hard,* and *Create Value.* You are responsible for creating the bridge from who you are now to where you want to be, and I have full faith that with *The Miracle Morning for College Students,* you will do just that.

Congratulations on starting your journey.

Sincerely,

Jeff Hoffman
Co-founder of Priceline.com
Co-founder of ColorJar

A NOTE FROM HAL

Welcome to the Miracle Morning. I think it's safe for us to say that there is at least one thing we have in common (probably a lot more than just one, but at least one that we know for sure): We want to improve our lives and ourselves. This is not to suggest that there is anything necessarily "wrong" with us or our lives, but as human beings we were born with the innate desire and drive to continuously grow and improve. I believe it's within all of us. Yet, most of us wake up each day, and life pretty much stays the same.

Whatever your life is like right now—whether you are currently experiencing extraordinary levels of success, enduring the most challenging time of your life, or somewhere in between—I can say with absolute certainty that the Miracle Morning is the most practical, results-oriented, and effective method I have ever encountered for improving **every** area of your life and doing so faster than you may believe is possible.

For college students, the Miracle Morning can be an absolute game-changer, allowing you to attain that elusive *next level* and take your personal and academic success far beyond what you've achieved up to this point. While this can include increasing your GPA or having a successful life after your college graduation, it's often more about discovering new ways to experience deeper levels of fulfillment and success in aspects of your life that you may have neglected. This can mean making significant improvements in your **health, happiness, relationships, finances, spirituality,** or any other areas that are at the top of your list.

For those who are in the midst of adversity and enduring times of struggle—be it mental, emotional, physical, financial, relational, or other—the Miracle Morning has proven time and time again to be the one thing that can empower anyone to overcome seemingly insurmountable challenges, make major breakthroughs, and turn their circumstances around, often in a short period of time.

Whether you want to make significant improvements in just a few key areas, or you are ready for a major overhaul that will radically transform your entire life—so that your current circumstances will soon become a memory of what was—you've picked up the right book. You are about to begin a miraculous journey using a simple, step-by-step process that is guaranteed to transform any area of your life ... all before 8:00 a.m.

I know, I know—these are some big promises to make. But the Miracle Morning is already generating measurable results for hundreds of thousands of people around the world, and it can absolutely be the one thing that takes you to where you want to be. My coauthors and I have done everything in our power to ensure that this book will be a truly life-changing investment of your time, energy, and attention. Thank you for allowing us to be a part of your life. Our miraculous journey together is about to begin.

With love & gratitude,

Hal

A NOTE FROM NATALIE

"No matter what people tell you, words and ideas can change the world."
—ROBIN WILLIAMS

Hello friend! I'm so glad you have picked up this book. Whatever point you are at in your life right now, I welcome you. When I was a student, I had so much to learn. Whether it was about class or about my own life, I always felt like I needed advice. There were many moments when I was scared, hopeless, and looking for answers. In the mornings when I woke up, my first words were usually a stream of expletives because I probably overslept and was late to my first class. Not exactly a pleasant way to wake up! For the rest of the day, I felt frantic, overwhelmed, and stressed. I absolutely did not like feeling out of control about my own life. I was usually procrastinating on my homework and had no motivation to do anything. Depression and anxiety began feeling normal to me. I was failing in every area of my life, but I refused to believe that that is how I wanted to live my life.

As a college student, The Miracle Morning was not about waking up early for me; rather, it was about *how* I started each day. Instead of cursing and resisting the obstacles I had coming my way, I welcomed each day with the spirit of gratitude. The morning routine gave me the time to take care of myself first before I started a busy day. It gave me the silence I needed to focus on my intentions and then tackle my day with confidence. My morning routine helped me improve my grades and the quality of my life. I was happy again! I felt empowered! I had the tools to design the life I wanted to live.

The Life S.A.V.E.R.S. truly saved my life, and it was all because I was lucky enough to have seen Hal Elrod speak when I was in high school. When I was struggling during college, I remembered Hal and how inspired he left me after he completed his talk. I looked up the book *The Miracle Morning* on Amazon and bought it, and I have never looked back since. I knew *The Miracle Morning* could help many college students, and it was my dream to coauthor this book. I am grateful to Hal and Honorée for making my dream of helping college students come true.

They say that people write the book they wish they had when they were struggling. That is certainly the case for me! This book will give you all the tools you need to get to the next level as a student and as an individual. College was a great time of fun, adventure, and personal growth. I want your college experience to be as defining and meaningful for you as it was for me!

This book will be your guide for the areas you want to improve in your life. Before you read any further, grab a pen or pencil so you can write in this book. Mark anything that stands out that you might want to come back to later. Underline, circle, highlight, fold the corners of pages, and take notes in the margins so you can quickly recall the most important lessons, ideas, and strategies when you return to them.

I invite you to join **The Miracle Morning for College Students** Facebook page. It will be your new go-to place to seek advice, support, and encouragement on your Miracle Morning journey. Introduce yourself on the page so we all get to know you. I am excited to see you there!

Finally, you may have many amazing professors during your time in college, but nothing will prove to be your greatest teacher more than your failures. Certainly, none of us wants to fail, but it happens even to those who want to succeed the most. So keep trying, keep succeeding, and keep failing. There is something to learn in all of those experiences. Do not fear failure, and more importantly, do not let your fear of failure stop you from achieving your goals. I believe you (yes, *you!*) are destined for greatness, and I want to help you get there. Now is your time to grow, to create opportunities, and to shine! Let's get this started, shall we?!

Your friend,
Natalie

SECTION I:

THE MIRACLE MORNING
+
LIFE S.A.V.E.R.S

— 1 —

WHY MORNINGS MATTER
(MORE THAN YOU THINK)

"'Life's too short' is repeated often enough to be a cliché, but this time it's true. You don't have enough time to be both unhappy and mediocre. It's not just pointless, it's painful."
—SETH GODIN,
New York Times best-selling author

"You've got to get up every morning with determination if you're going to go to bed with satisfaction."
—GEORGE LORIMER,
American journalist and author

How you start each morning sets your mindset and the context for the rest of your day. Start every day with a purposeful, disciplined, growth-infused, and goal-oriented morning, and you're virtually guaranteed to crush your day.

Do you start your day feeling overwhelmed? I'd be willing to bet that most college students do. In fact, many snooze through their alarms. Their day starts when they must get out of bed or when they are already running late for class.

What if you could have that time of peace and quiet you've been dreaming about? That clean, uncluttered mental space where you could regain your sense of elegance and dignity, where you're in total control and can proceed in an orderly, self-nurturing fashion? But you know you can't—or maybe you can but not today. Maybe when you have slept enough, or when you do not have a lot of papers to write or exams to study for.

It's no wonder most college students start their days with resistance, letting how they are feeling or their responsibilities set the agenda, and sending a message to their subconscious minds that says they don't have enough energy or even the will to get out of bed. They think today will be another free-for-all where their personal goals go out the window in the usual scramble that is college.

Add to this the fact that most college students believe they aren't early risers, and the pattern of procrastination shows up early in life.

But what if you could change it?

What if, when the alarm clock starts beeping in the morning, you could consider it to be life's first gift? It's the gift of time that you can dedicate to becoming the person you need to be to achieve all of your goals and dreams—for yourself and everyone you care for—while the rest of the world is still asleep.

You might be thinking, All of this sounds great, Natalie. *But. I. Am. Not. A. Morning. Person.*

I understand. I really do! You're not saying anything I haven't told myself a thousand times before. And believe me, I tried—and failed— many times to take control of my mornings. But that was before I discovered *The Miracle Morning.*

Stay with me here. In addition to wanting academic success, I bet you also want to stop putting so much pressure on yourself, comparing yourself to others, and missing the goals you have set for yourself. You want to release the intense and not-so-great emotions that go along with those challenges. These things get in the way of being a successful college student, because they affect your self-esteem and prevent you from feeling good about yourself and your life.

I'm a firm believer in the advice given at the start of every airplane flight: Put your own oxygen mask on first, and then help your child. You won't be able to help anyone if you pass out due to lack of oxygen.

Many students don't see this simple truth. They think that success means putting your own needs last, and they have so much to do that they never get to those needs. Over time, they end up overcommitted, exhausted, depressed, resentful, and overwhelmed.

Sound familiar?

Then know this:

Mornings are the key to it all.

More important than even the *time* that you start your day is the *mindset* with which you start your day.

Although there's a chance you're reading this book after years of being stressed, there's also a good chance that you're reading this book in the early stages, which means that you may be feeling overwhelmed and looking for answers. If that's the case, then learning to practice your Miracle Morning before anything else is important to make sure you get *your time*, uninterrupted. The good news is … it's worth it, and it is far more fun and rewarding than you might expect.

But, before I get into exactly *how* you can master your mornings, let me make the case for *why*. Because, believe me, once you've uncovered the profound truth about mornings, you'll never want to miss one again.

WHY MORNINGS MATTER SO MUCH

The more you explore the power of early rising and morning rituals, the more proof mounts that the early bird gets *a lot* more than the worm. Here are just a few of the key advantages you're about to experience for yourself:

You'll have a better GPA.

A study conducted at The University of North Texas in 2008 titled "Morningness a Predictor of Better Grades in College" revealed that college students who identified themselves as "early birds" had GPAs a full point higher than those who were "night owls" (3.5 GPA vs. 2.5 GPA). Its findings were published in the *American Academy of Sleep Medicine,* within which Dr. Daniel Taylor, the professor who led this study, said that being a morning person was worth a "full letter grade difference" for college students.

You'll be more proactive and productive.

Christoph Randler is a professor of biology at the University of Education in Heidelberg, Germany. In the July 2010 issue of *Harvard Business Review,* Randler shared his finding that "People whose performance peaks in the morning are better positioned for career success, because they're more proactive than people who are at their best in the evening." According to New York Times best-selling author and world-renowned entrepreneur Robin Sharma, "If you study many of the most productive people in the world, they all had one thing in common—they were early risers."

You'll anticipate problems and head them off at the pass.

Randler went on to surmise that morning people hold all of the important cards. They are "better able to anticipate and minimize problems, are proactive, have greater professional success, and ultimately make higher wages." He noted that morning people are able to anticipate problems and handle them with grace and ease. If you think about it, this could be the key to decreasing the level of stress that inevitably comes with being a college student.

You'll plan like a pro.

Planning is very important to exceptional college students. It's been said that *when we fail to plan, we are indirectly planning to fail.* Morning folks have the time to organize, anticipate, and prepare for their day. Our sleepy counterparts are reactive, leaving a lot to chance. Aren't you more stressed when you sleep through your alarm? Getting up with the sun (or before) lets you jump-start your day. While everyone else is running around trying and failing to get their day under control, you'll be more calm, cool, and collected.

You'll have more energy.

One component of your new Miracle Mornings will be morning exercise, which is something often neglected by busy college students. Yet, in as little as a few minutes, exercise sets a positive tone for the day. Increased blood to the brain will help you think more clearly and focus on what's most important. Fresh oxygen will permeate every cell in your body and increase your energy, which is why college students who exercise are in a better mood and in better shape, getting better sleep, and being more productive.

You'll gain early-bird attitude advantages.

Recently, researchers at the University of Barcelona in Spain compared morning people, those early birds who like to get up at dawn, with evening people, night owls who prefer to stay up late and sleep in. Among the differences, they found that morning people tend to be more persistent and resistant to fatigue, frustration, and difficulties. That translates into lower levels of anxiety, rates of depression, and likelihood of substance abuse—but higher life satisfaction. Sounds good to me! A better attitude has helped me create a more powerful mindset, which made me a better college student, and has helped me create personal success in my life after graduating college.

The evidence is in, and the experts have had their say. *Mornings contain the secret to an extraordinarily successful life.*

MORNINGS? REALLY?

I admit it. To go from *I'm not a morning person* to *I really want to become a morning person* to *I'm up early every morning, and it feels amazing!* is a process. But after some trial and error, you will discover how to outfox, preempt, and foil your inner late sleeper so you can make early rising a habit.

Okay, sounds great in theory, but you might be shaking your head and telling yourself, *There's no way. I'm already cramming 27 hours of stuff into 24 hours. How on earth could I get up an hour earlier than I already do?*

Let me ask you, *How can you not?*

The key thing to understand is that the Miracle Morning isn't about denying yourself another hour of sleep so you can have an even longer, harder day. It's not even about waking up earlier. It's about waking up *better*.

Thousands of people around the planet are already living their own Miracle Mornings. Many of them were night owls. But they're making it work. In fact, they're *thriving*. And it's not because they simply added an hour to their day. It's because they added *the right* hour. And so can you.

Still skeptical? Then let me tell you this: *The hardest part about getting up an hour earlier is the first five minutes.* That's the crucial time when, tucked into your warm bed, you make the decision to start your day or hit the snooze button *just one more time*. It's the moment of truth, and the decision you make right then will change your day, your success, and your life.

And that's why the first five minutes is the starting point for *The Miracle Morning for College Students*. It's time for you to win every morning! When we win our mornings, we win the day.

In the next two chapters, I'll make waking up early easier and more exciting than it's ever been in your life (even if you've *never* considered yourself to be a morning person), and show you how to maximize those newfound morning minutes with the Life S.A.V.E.R.S.—the six most powerful and proven personal development practices known to man.

Chapters 4, 5, and 6 will reveal not-so-obvious college student principles related to accelerating your personal growth, why you needto structure your life to gain endless amounts of energy, and how to optimize your ability to stay focused on your goals and what matters most.

Finally, chapters 7, 8, 9, and 10 cover the critical skills you must master to become an exceptional college student, and chapter 11 gives you a 30-day challenge that will jump-start your Miracle Morning habits so you can achieve those results. There's even a final bonus chapter from Hal that I think you are going to love!

We have a lot of ground to cover in this book, so let's jump right in.

— 2 —

IT ONLY TAKES FIVE MINUTES TO BECOME A MORNING PERSON

*If you really think about it, hitting the snooze button in the morning
doesn't even make sense. It's like saying, "I hate
getting up in the morning, so I do it over,
and over, and over again."*

—DEMETRI MARTIN, Comedian

Have you ever considered that how we start our day could be single most important factor in determining how we live our lives? When we wake up with excitement and create a purposeful, powerful, productive morning, we set ourselves up to win the day.

Yet, most people start their day with resistance and procrastination, hitting the snooze button and waiting until the last possible moment to pry themselves out from beneath their cozy covers. While it may not be obvious, this seemingly innocent act may be sending a detrimental message to their subconscious minds, programming their psyche with the unconscious belief that they don't have the self-discipline to get out of bed in the morning, let alone do what's necessary to achieve everything else they want for their lives.

Could it be that how we wake up in the morning affects who we're becoming, and thus changes every area of our lives?

When the alarm clock starts beeping in the morning, consider that as life's first *gift, challenge,* and *opportunity* to us—all three at the same time—each day. It's the gift of another day, the challenge of making the disciplined decision to get out of bed, and the opportunity to invest time in our personal development so each of us can become the person we need to be to create the life we truly want. And we get to do all of this while the rest of the world continues to sleep.

However, if it weren't for this strategy that you're about to learn, I'd still be snoozing through my alarm clock every morning and clinging to my old limiting belief that I was *not a morning person.*

The good news is that it is possible to love waking up—and do it easily each day—even if you've *never* been a morning person.

I know you might not believe it. Right now you think, *That might be true for early birds, but trust me, I've tried. I'm just not a morning person.*

But it is true. I know because I've been there. I used to sleep until the last possible moment, when I absolutely had to wake up. And even then, it took me a while to get out of bed. I was a "snooze-aholic," as Hal calls them. I dreaded mornings. I hated waking up.

And now I love it.

How did I do it? When people ask me how I transformed myself into a morning person—and transformed my life in the process—I tell them I did it in five simple steps, one at a time. I know it may seem downright impossible. But take it from a former snooze-aholic: you can do this. And you can do it the same way I did.

That's the critical message about waking up—it's possible to change. Morning people aren't born—they're self-made. You can do it, and it doesn't require the willpower of an Olympic marathoner. I contend that when early rising becomes not only something you do, but *who you are,* you will truly love mornings. Waking up will become for you like it is for me—effortless.

Not convinced? Suspend your disbelief a little and let me introduce you to the five-step process that changed my life. Five simple, snooze-proof keys that made waking up in the morning—even early in the morning—easier than ever before. Without this strategy, I would still be sleeping (or snoozing) through the alarm(s) each morning. Worse, I would still be clinging to the limiting belief that I am not a morning person.

And I would have missed a whole world of opportunity.

THE CHALLENGE WITH WAKING UP

Waking up earlier is a bit like running: You think you're not a runner—maybe you even *hate* running—until you lace up a pair of running shoes and reluctantly head out the front door at a pace that suggests you might be about to go for a run. With a commitment to overcome your seemingly insurmountable disdain for running, you put one foot in front of the other. Do this for a few weeks, and one day it hits you: *I've become a runner.*

Similarly, if you've resisted waking up in the morning and chosen to hit the *Procrastination* button—I mean *Snooze* button, then of course you're not *yet* a morning person. But follow the simple step-by-step process that you're about to discover, and you'll wake up in a few weeks (maybe even a few days) and it will hit you: *OMG, I can't believe it … I've become a morning person!*

The possibilities feel amazing right now, and you might be feeling motivated, excited, and optimistic. But what happens tomorrow morning when that alarm goes off? How motivated will you be when you're yanked out of a deep sleep by a screaming alarm clock?

We all know where motivation will be right then. It will be flushed down the toilet, replaced by rationalization. And rationalization is a crafty master—in seconds, we can convince ourselves that we need just a few extra minutes … and the next thing we know, we're scrambling around the house late for class, late for work, late for life. Again.

It's a tricky problem. Just when we need our motivation the most—those first few moments of the day—is precisely when we seem to have the least of it.

The solution is to boost that morning motivation and mount a surprise attack on rationalization. That's what the five steps that follow do for you. Each step in the process is designed to increase what Hal calls your Wake Up Motivation Level (WUML).

First thing in the morning, you might have a low WUML, meaning you want nothing more than to go back to sleep when your alarm goes off. That's normal. But by using this simple five-step process (which takes about five minutes), you can generate a high WUML that makes you ready to jump up and embrace the day.

THE FIVE-STEP, SNOOZE-PROOF WAKE-UP STRATEGY

Minute One: Set Your Intentions *Before Bed*

The first key to waking up is to understand this: *Your first thought in the morning is usually the same as your last thought before you went to sleep.* I bet, for example, that you've had nights where you could hardly fall asleep because you were so excited about waking up the next morning. Whether it was when you were a kid on Christmas morning, or the day you were leaving for a big vacation, as soon as the alarm sounded, you opened your eyes ready to jump out of bed. Why? It's because the last thought you had about the coming morning—before you fell asleep—was positive.

On the other hand, if your last thought before bed is, "Oh gosh, I can't believe I have to get up in six hours—I'm going to be exhausted in the morning!" then your first thought when the alarm clock goes off is likely to be something like, "Oh gosh, it's already been six hours? Nooo … I just want to keep sleeping!" Consider that it is a self-fulfilling prophecy and that you create your own reality.

The first step is to consciously decide—every night, before bed—to actively and mindfully create a positive expectation for the next morning. Visualize it and affirm it to yourself.

For help on this and to get the precise words to say before bed to create your powerful morning intentions, download "The Miracle Morning Bedtime Affirmations" free at www.TMMBook.com.

Minute Two: Move Your Alarm Clock Across the Room

If you haven't already, be sure to move your alarm clock as far away from your bed as possible. This will make it so you have to actually get out of bed and engage your body in movement to start each day. Motion creates energy, and getting out of bed and walking across the room naturally helps you to wake up.

Most people keep their alarm clock next to their bed. Think about it: If you keep your alarm clock within reach, then you're still in a partial sleep state after the alarm goes off, and your wake up motivation level (aka your WUML) is at its lowest point, which makes it much more difficult to summon the discipline to get out of bed. In fact, you may turn off the alarm without even realizing it! On more than a few occasions, we've all convinced ourselves that our alarm clock was merely part of the dream we were having. (You're not alone on that one, trust me.)

By forcing yourself to get out of bed to turn off the alarm, you are setting yourself up for early-rising success by instantly increasing your WUML.

However, on a scale of one to ten, your WUML may still be hovering around five, and you'll likely be feeling more sleepy than not, so the temptation to turn around and crawl back into bed will still be present. To raise that WUML just a little further, try ...

Minute Three: Brush Your Teeth

As soon as you've gotten out of bed and turned off your alarm clock, go directly to the bathroom sink to brush your teeth. I know what you may be thinking. *Really? You're telling me that I need to brush my teeth?* Yes. The point is that you're doing mindless activities for the first few minutes and giving your body time to wake up.

After turning off your alarm, go directly to the bathroom sink to brush your teeth and splash some warm (or cold) water on your face. This simple activity will allow for the passing of more time to increase your WUML even further.

Now that your mouth is minty fresh, it's time to …

Minute Four: Drink a Full Glass of Water

It's crucial that you hydrate yourself first thing every morning. After six to eight hours without water, you'll be mildly dehydrated, which causes fatigue. Often when people feel tired—at any time of day—what they really need is more water, not more sleep.

Start by getting a glass or bottle of water (or you can do what I do, and fill it up the night before so it's already there for you in the morning) and drinking it as fast as is comfortable for you. The objective is to replace the water you were deprived of during the hours you slept. (And hey, the side benefits of morning hydration include better, younger-looking skin and maintaining a healthy weight. Not bad for a few ounces of water!)

That glass of water should raise your WUML another notch, which will get you to …

Minute Five: Get Dressed in Your Workout Clothes (or Jump in the Shower)

The fifth step has two options. *Option one* is to get dressed in your exercise clothing so you're ready to leave your bedroom and immediately engage in your Miracle Morning. You can lay out your clothes before you go to bed or sleep in your workout clothes. (Yes, really.) And for college students, prep you do the night before is especially important to help you go straight into your practice. You can make this part of your bedtime ritual.

Option two is to jump in the shower, which is a great way to take your WUML to the point where staying awake is much easier. However, I usually opt to change into exercise clothes, since I'll need a shower after working out, and I believe there is something to be said for *earning* your morning shower! But a lot of people prefer their shower first because it helps them wake up and gives them a fresh start to the day. The choice is completely yours.

Regardless of which option you choose, by the time you've executed these five simple steps, your WUML should be high enough that it requires very little discipline to stay awake for your Miracle Morning.

If you were to try to make that commitment the moment your alarm first went off—while you were at a WUML of nearly zero—it would be a much more difficult decision to make. The five steps let you build momentum so that, within just a few minutes, you're ready to go instead of feeling groggy.

I have never made it through the first five minutes and decided to go back to bed. Once I am up and moving with intention through the morning, I can more easily continue being purposeful throughout the day.

MIRACLE MORNING BONUS WAKE-UP TIPS

Although this strategy has worked for thousands of people, these five steps are not the only way to make waking up in the morning easier. Here are a few others I've heard from fellow Miracle Morning practitioners:

1. "The Miracle Morning Bedtime Affirmations": If you haven't done this yet, take a moment now to go to www.TMMbook. com and download the energizing, intention-setting "Bedtime Affirmations" for free. Nothing is more effective for ensuring that you will wake up before your alarm than programming your mind to achieve exactly what you want.

2. Set a timer for your bedroom lights: One member of the Miracle Morning Community shared that he sets his bedroom lights on a timer (you can buy an appliance timer online or at your local hardware store). As his alarm goes off, the lights come on in the room. What a great idea! It's a lot easier to

fall back to sleep when it's dark—having the lights on tells your mind and body that it's time to wake up. Regardless of whether you use a timer, be sure to turn your light on first thing when your alarm goes off.

3. Set a timer for your bedroom heater: Another member of the Miracle Morning Community says that, in the winter, she keeps a bedroom heater on an appliance timer set to go off fifteen minutes before she wakes up. She keeps it cold at night, but warm for waking up so she won't be tempted to crawl back under her covers.

Feel free to add to or customize the five-minute, snooze-proof wake-up strategy, and if you have any tips that you're open to sharing, we'd love to hear them. Please post them in the Miracle Morning Community at www.MyTMMCommunity.com.

Waking up consistently and easily is all about having an effective, predetermined, step-by-step strategy to increase your WUML in the morning. Don't wait to try this! Start tonight by reading "The Miracle Morning Bedtime Affirmations" to set a powerful intention for waking up tomorrow morning, move your alarm clock across the room, set a glass of water on your nightstand, and commit to the other two steps for the morning.

TAKING IMMEDIATE ACTION

There's no need to wait to get started implementing the power of early rising. As Tony Robbins has said, "When is NOW a good time for you to do that?" Now, indeed, would be perfect! In fact, the sooner you start, the sooner you'll begin to see results, including increased energy, a better attitude, and, of course, a happier home life.

Step One: Set your alarm for 30–60 minutes earlier than you usually wake up, for the next 30 days. That's it; just 30–60 minutes for 30 days, starting now. And be sure to write into your schedule to do your first Miracle Morning … *tomorrow morning*. That's right, don't using *waiting until you finish the book* as an excuse to procrastinate on getting started!

If you're feeling resistant at all, because maybe you've tried to make changes in the past but haven't followed through, here's a suggestion: Turn now to Chapter 11 and read ahead about the 30-Day Miracle Morning Challenge. This will give you not only the mindset and strategy to overcome any resistance you may have to getting started, but also the most effective process for implementing a new habit and sticking with it. Think of it as beginning with the end in mind.

From this day forward, starting with the next 30 days, keep your alarm set for 30–60 minutes earlier than you typically wake up so that you can start waking up when you *want* to, instead of when you *have* to. It's time to start launching each day with a Miracle Morning so that you can become the person you need to be to take yourself and your academics to extraordinary levels.

What will you do with that hour? You're going to find out in the next chapter, but for now simply continue reading this book during your Miracle Morning until you learn the whole routine.

Step Two: Join the Miracle Morning Community at www. MyTMMCommunity.com to connect with and get support from more than 80,000 like-minded early risers, many of whom have been generating extraordinary results with the Miracle Morning for years.

Step Three: Find a Miracle Morning accountability partner. Enroll someone—a roommate, friend, family member, co-worker, or someone you meet in the Miracle Morning Community—to join you on this adventure so you can encourage, support, and hold each other accountable to follow through until your Miracle Morning has become part of who you are.

Okay, now let's get into the six most powerful, proven, personal development practices known to man (or woman) ... The Life S.A.V.E.R.S.

— 3 —
THE LIFE S.A.V.E.R.S.

Six Practices Guaranteed to Save You from a Life of Unfulfilled Potential

What Hal has done with his acronym S.A.V.E.R.S. is take the best practices—developed over centuries of human consciousness development—and condensed the "best of the best" into a daily morning ritual. A ritual that is now part of my day.

Many people do one of the S.A.V.E.R.S. daily. For example, many people do the E, they exercise every morning. Others do S for silence or meditation, or S for scribing or journaling. But until Hal packaged S.A.V.E.R.S., no one was doing all six ancient "best practices" every morning. The Miracle Morning is perfect for very busy, successful people. Going through S.A.V.E.R.S. every morning is like pumping rocket fuel into my body, mind, and spirit ... before I start my day, every day.

—ROBERT KIYOSAKI, Best-Selling author of *Rich Dad Poor Dad*

Most people live their lives on the wrong side of a significant gap that separates *who we are* from *who we can become*, which holds us back from creating the life we truly want. Often we become frustrated with ourselves and our lack of consistent motivation, effort, and results in one or more areas of life. We spend too much time *thinking* about the actions we should take to create the results we want, but then we don't take those actions. More often than not, we know what we need to do ... we just don't consistently do what we know.

Do you ever feel like that? Like the life and success that you want, and the person you know you need to be to create both, are just beyond your grasp? When you see other college students who are excelling in an area, or playing at a level that you're not, does it ever seem like they've got it all figured out? Like they must know something you don't because if you knew it then you'd be excelling, too?

When Hal experienced the second of his two rock bottoms (the first was when he died for six minutes in a car crash, and the second was when his business failed due to the financial collapse of 2008), he felt lost and depressed. He tried to apply what he already knew wasn't working. Nothing he tried was improving his situation. So, he began his own quest for the fastest, most effective strategy to take his success to the next level. He went in search of the best personal development practices that were being practiced by the world's most successful people.

After discovering and assembling a list of six of the most timeless, effective, and proven personal development practices, he first attempted to determine which one or two would accelerate his success the fastest. However, his breakthrough occurred when he asked himself, *what would happen if I did ALL of these?*

So, he did. Within just two months of implementing all six practices, nearly every single day, Hal experienced what you might call miraculous results. He was able to more than double his income, and he went from someone who had never run more than a mile, to training to run a 52-mile ultramarathon—because he *wasn't* a runner and actually despised running. He thought *What better way to take his physical, mental, emotional, and spiritual capacities to another level?*

So, whether you're already very successful, like multimillionaire entrepreneur Robert Kiyosaki (who practices the Miracle Morning and the Life S.A.V.E.R.S. almost every day), or if you've ever felt like the life you want to live, and the person you know you can be, are just beyond your grasp, the Life S.A.V.E.R.S. are virtually guaranteed to save you from missing out on the extraordinary life you truly want.

WHY THE LIFE S.A.V.E.R.S. WORK

The Life S.A.V.E.R.S. are simple but profoundly effective daily morning practices that are virtually guaranteed to enable you to become more so that you can fulfill your potential. They also give you space to gain heightened levels of clarity to plan and live your life on your terms. They're designed to start your day by putting you in a peak physical, mental, emotional, and spiritual state so you continually improve, and so you will feel great and *always* perform at your best.

I know, I know. You don't have time. Before starting the Miracle Morning, I would wake up to pure chaos with barely enough time to get dressed and out the door to class or work. You probably think you can hardly squeeze in what you have to do already, never mind what you want to do. But I "didn't have time" before the Miracle Morning, either. And yet here I am with more time, more prosperity, and a more peaceful life than I've ever had.

What you need to realize right now is that your Miracle Morning will create time for you. The Life S.A.V.E.R.S. are the vehicle to help you reconnect with your true essence and wake up with purpose instead of obligation. The practices help you build energy, see priorities more clearly, and find the most productive flow in your life.

In other words, the Life S.A.V.E.R.S. don't take time from your day, but ultimately add more to it.

Each letter in Life S.A.V.E.R.S. represents one of the best practices of the most successful people on the planet. From A-list movie stars and world-class professional athletes to CEOs and entrepreneurs, you'd be hard pressed to find an elite performer who didn't swear by at least one of the S.A.V.E.R.S.

However, you'd be equally hard pressed to find an elite performer who practices even half—let alone *all* the Life S.A.V.E.R.S. (Well, I guess that's changing now that Hal has introduced the world to *The Miracle Morning*). That's what makes the Miracle Morning so effective:

You're harnessing the game-changing benefits of not just one, but all six of *the best practices, developed over centuries of human consciousness development* and combining them into a concise, fully customizable morning ritual.

The Life S.A.V.E.R.S. are:

Silence

Affirmations

Visualization

Exercise

Reading

Scribing

Leveraging these six practices is how you will accelerate your personal development during your newfound Miracle Morning ritual. They're customizable to fit you, your lifestyle, your business, and your specific goals. And you can start implementing them first thing tomorrow morning.

Let's go through each of the Life S.A.V.E.R.S. in detail.

"S" IS FOR SILENCE

Silence, the first practice of the Life S.A.V.E.R.S., is a key habit for college students. If you've been guilty of starting your day by immediately grabbing your phone or computer and diving into email, phone calls, social media, or text messages, then this is your opportunity to learn the power of beginning each day with peaceful, purposeful *silence*.

Like we did before the Miracle Morning, most people start the day when they *must* get out of bed. And most people run from morning to night, struggling to regain control for the rest of the day. It's not a coincidence. Starting each day with a period of silence instead will immediately reduce your stress levels and help you begin the day with the kind of calm and clarity that you need to focus on what's most important.

Remember, many of the world's most successful people are daily practitioners of silence. That shows you how important it is. It's not surprising that Oprah practices stillness—or that she does nearly all the other Life S.A.V.E.R.S., too. Musician Katy Perry practices transcendental meditation, as do Sheryl Crow and Sir Paul McCartney. Film and television stars Jennifer Aniston, Ellen DeGeneres, Jerry Seinfeld, Howard Stern, Cameron Diaz, Clint Eastwood, and Hugh Jackman have all spoken of their daily meditation practices. Hip-hop mogul Russell Simmons meditates with his two daughters every morning for 20 minutes. Even famous billionaires Ray Dalio and Rupert Murdoch have attributed their financial success to the daily practice of stillness. You'll be in good (and quiet) company by doing the same.

If it seems like I'm asking you to do nothing, let me clarify: you have a number of choices for your practice of silence. In no particular order, here are a few to get you started:

- Meditation
- Prayer
- Reflection
- Deep breathing
- Gratitude

Whichever you choose, be sure you don't stay in bed for your period of silence, and better still, get out of your bedroom altogether.

In an interview with *Shape Magazine*, actress and singer Kristen Bell said, "Do meditative yoga for 10 minutes every morning. When you have a problem—whether it's road rage, your guy, or work—meditation allows everything to unfold the way it's supposed to."

And don't be afraid to expand your horizons. Meditation comes in many forms. As Angelina Jolie told *Stylist Magazine*, "I find meditation in sitting on the floor with the kids coloring for an hour, or going on the trampoline. You do what you love, that makes you happy, and that gives you your meditation."

The Benefits of Silence

How many times do you find yourself stressed? How often do you have so much work that you do not have time to create a vision or plan? Daily! Having detrimental levels of stress and anxiety are the most common reasons why students cannot academically perform their very best. We face the ever-present distractions of other commitments encroaching on our schedule and the inevitable fires we must extinguish. Lots of people have the uncanny ability to push our stress buttons as well. They demand our time and attention even though those resources are scarce to you as a student.

Excessive stress is terrible for your health. It triggers your fight-or-flight response, and that releases a cascade of toxic hormones that can stay in your body for days. That's fine … if you experience that type of stress only occasionally.

According to Christopher Bergland, a world-record-holding triathlete, coach, and author, "The stress hormone, cortisol, is public health enemy number one. Scientists have known for years that elevated cortisol levels: interfere with learning and memory, lower immune function and bone density, increase weight gain, blood pressure, cholesterol, heart disease ... The list goes on and on. Chronic stress and elevated cortisol levels also increase risk for depression, mental illness, and lower life expectancy."

Silence in the form of meditation reduces stress, and, as a result, improves your health. A major study run by several groups, including the National Institutes of Health, the American Medical Association, the Mayo Clinic, and scientists from both Harvard and Stanford, revealed that meditation reduces stress and high blood pressure. A recent study by Dr. Norman Rosenthal, a world-renowned psychiatrist who works with the David Lynch Foundation, even found that people who practice meditation are 30 percent less likely to die from heart disease.

Another study from Harvard found that ju
meditation could lead to "increased gray-mat
hippocampus, known to be important for lea
and in structures associated with self-awareness,
and introspection."

Meditation helps you to slow down and focus on you, even if it's for just a short time. Start your meditation practice and say goodbye to feeling scattered and wandering aimlessly without intention and purpose through your day.

"I started meditating because I felt like I needed to stop my life from running me," singer Sheryl Crow has said. "So meditation for me helped slow my day down." She continues to devote 20 minutes in the morning and 20 minutes at night to meditation.

When you are silent, it opens a space for you before you encounter anyone else. The benefits are extraordinary and can bring you much-needed clarity and peace of mind so you bring your best self to any interaction. Practicing silence, in other words, can help you reduce your stress, improve cognitive performance, and become confident at the same time.

Guided Meditations and Meditation Apps

Meditation is like anything else: If you've never done it before, it can be difficult or feel awkward at first. If you are a first-time meditator, I recommend starting with a guided meditation.

Here are a few of my favorite meditation apps that are available for both iPhone/iPad and Android devices:

- Headspace
- Brightmind
- Calm
- Omvana
- Simply Being
- Insight Timer

_here are subtle and significant differences among these meditation ps, one of which is the voice of the person speaking. Experiment and choose what works best for you.

If you don't have a device that allows you to download apps, simply go to YouTube or Google and search for the keywords "Guided Meditation." You can also search by duration (e.g., "five-minute guided meditation") or topic (e.g., "guided meditation for increased confidence").

Miracle Morning (Individual) Meditation

When you're ready to try meditating on your own, here is a simple, step-by-step meditation you can use during your Miracle Morning, even if you've never done this before.

1. Before beginning, it's important to prepare yourself and set expectations. This is a time for you to quiet your mind and let go of the compulsive need to be thinking about something—reliving the past or worrying about the future, but never living fully in the present. This is the time to let go of your stresses, take a break from worrying about your problems, and be here in this moment. It is a time to access the essence of who you truly are, to go deeper than what you have, what you do, or the labels you've accepted as who you are. If this sounds foreign to you, or too new agey, that's okay. I've felt the same way. It's probably because you've never tried it before. But thankfully, you're about to.

2. Find a quiet, comfortable place to sit, on the couch, on a chair, on the floor, or on a pillow for added comfort.

3. Sit upright, cross-legged. You can close your eyes, or you can look down at a point on the ground about two feet in front of you.

4. Begin by focusing on your breath, taking slow, deep breaths. Breathe in through the nose and out through the mouth. The

most effective breathing causes your belly to expand and not your chest.

5. Now start pacing your breath. Breathe in slowly for a count of three seconds (one one thousand, two one thousand, three one thousand), hold it in for another three counts, and then breathe out slowly for a final count of three. Notice your thoughts and emotions settling down as you focus on your breath. Be aware that, as you attempt to quiet your mind, thoughts will still come in to pay a visit. Simply acknowledge them and let them go, always returning your focus to the breath.

6. Allow yourself to be fully present in this moment. Some people refer to this state as *being*. Not thinking, not doing, just being. Continue to follow your breath and imagine inhaling positive, loving, and peaceful energy and exhaling all your worries and stress. Enjoy the quiet. Enjoy the moment. Just breathe ... Just be.

7. If you find that you have a constant influx of thoughts, it may be helpful for you to focus on a single word, phrase, or mantra to repeat to yourself as you inhale and exhale. For example, you might try something like this: "I inhale confidence ..." (on the inhale) "I exhale fear ..." (as you exhale). You can swap the word confidence for whatever you feel you need to bring more of into your life (love, faith, energy, strength, etc.), and swap the word fear with whatever you feel you need to let go of (stress, worry, resentment, etc.).

Meditation is a gift you can give yourself every day. My time spent meditating has become one of my favorite parts of the Miracle Morning routine. It's a time to be at peace and to experience gratitude and freedom from my day-to-day stressors and worries.

Think of daily meditation as a temporary vacation from the challenges of life. Although your problems will still be there when you finish each day, you'll find that you're more centered and better equipped to solve them.

"A" IS FOR AFFIRMATIONS

Have you ever wondered how some people seem to be good at *everything* they do and consistently achieve at a level so high, you can hardly comprehend how you're ever going to join them? Or why others seem to drop every ball? Time and time again, it is a person's *mindset* that has proven to be the driving factor in their results.

Mindset is the accumulation of beliefs, attitude, and emotional intelligence. In her bestselling book, *Mindset: The New Psychology of Success*, Carol Dweck, Ph.D., explains it this way: "For twenty years, my research has shown that the view you adopt of yourself profoundly affects the way you lead your life."

Others can easily sense your mindset. It shows up undeniably in your language, your confidence, and your demeanor. Your mindset affects everything! Show me someone with a successful mindset, and I'll show you a successful college student.

I know firsthand, though, how difficult it can be to maintain the right mindset—the confidence and enthusiasm, not to mention motivation—during the roller-coaster ride that comes with being a college student. Mindset is largely something we adopt without conscious thought. At a subconscious level, we have been programmed to think, believe, act, and talk to ourselves a certain way.

Our programming comes from many influences, including what others have told us, what we repeat to ourselves, and all of our good and bad life experiences. That programming expresses itself in every area of our lives, including the way we are in school, which means that, if we want to be better at our academics, we need to upgrade our mental programming.

Affirmations are a tool for doing just that. They enable you to become more intentional about your goals while also providing the encouragement and positive mindset necessary to achieve them.

Science has proven that affirmations—when done correctly—are one of the most effective tools for quickly becoming the person you need to be to achieve everything you want in your life—for yourself, your academics, and your relationships. And yet affirmations also get a bad rap. Many people have tried them only to be disappointed with little or no results. You can, however, leverage affirmations in a way that will absolutely produce results for you. I'll show you how.

By repeatedly articulating and reinforcing to yourself *what* result you want to accomplish, *why* accomplishing it is important to you, *which* specific actions are required to produce that result, and, most importantly, precisely *when* you commit to taking those actions, your subconscious mind will shift your beliefs and behavior. You'll begin to automatically believe and act in new ways, and eventually manifest your affirmations into your reality. But first ...

Why the Old Way of Doing Affirmations Doesn't Work

For decades, countless so-called experts and gurus have taught affirmations in ways that have proven to be ineffective and set people up for failure. Here are two of the most common problems with affirmations.

Problem #1: Lying to Yourself Doesn't Work

I have a 4.0 GPA. Really?

I have 7 percent body fat. Do you?

I have achieved all of my goals this year. Have you?

Creating affirmations as if you've already become or achieved something may be the single biggest cause of affirmations not being effective for most people.

With this technique, every time you recite the affirmation that isn't rooted in truth, your subconscious resists it. You're an intelligent human being who isn't delusional, so lying to yourself repeatedly will never be the optimum strategy. *The truth will always prevail.*

Problem #2: Passive Language Doesn't Produce Results

Many affirmations are designed to make you feel good by creating an empty promise of something you desire. For example, here is a popular money affirmation that's been perpetuated by many:

I am a money magnet. Money flows to me effortlessly and in abundance.

This type of affirmation might make you feel good in the moment by giving you a false sense of relief from your financial worries, but it won't generate any income. People who sit back and wait for money to show up magically are cash-poor.

To generate the kind of abundance you want (or any result you desire, for that matter), you've got to actually do something. Your actions must be in alignment with your desired results, and your affirmations must articulate and affirm both.

Four Steps to Create Miracle Morning Affirmations (That Produce Results)

Here are four simple steps to create and implement results-oriented Miracle Morning affirmations that will program your subconscious mind while directing your conscious mind to upgrade your behavior, so that you begin to produce results and take your levels of personal and academic success beyond what you've ever experienced before.

Step One: The Ideal Result You Are Committed to and Why

Notice I'm not starting with what you *want*. Everyone wants things, but we don't get what we want: we get what we're committed to. You want to be a great college student? Who doesn't? Join that nonexclusive club. Oh wait, you're 100 percent committed to becoming a successful student by clarifying and executing the necessary actions until the result is achieved? Okay, now we're talking.

Action: Start by writing down a specific, extraordinary result or outcome—one that challenges you and would significantly improve your life, and one that you are ready to commit to creating—even if you're not yet sure how you will do it. Then reinforce your commitment by including your *why*, the compelling reason you're willing to stay committed.

I am dedicated to make a list of next week's homework assignments every Thursday and choose one to complete early so that I can have a more relaxing weekend with friends and a less stressful week the following week.

Or …

I am 100 percent committed to being as healthy as I can be so that I have the energy to be fully present in my classes and my work.

Or …

I am committed to improving my grades by one letter grade in the next quarter/semester, from _____ to _____, so that I can improve my skills as a student and improve my GPA in the process.

Step Two: The Necessary Actions You Are Committed to Taking and When

Writing an affirmation that merely affirms what you *want* without affirming what you are committed to *doing* is one step above pointless and can actually be counterproductive by tricking your subconscious mind into thinking that the result will happen automatically and without effort.

Action: Clarify the (specific) action, activity, or habit that is required for you to achieve your ideal outcome, and clearly state when and how often you will execute the necessary action.

To ensure that I manage my stress, I am committed to completing assignments early. To accomplish that, I am committed to block a half hour per week to write down all the assignments that I know are due the following week and then choose the assignment(s) I will complete before the next academic week begins.

Or …

To ensure that I am as healthy as I can be, I am 100 percent committed to going to the gym five days per week and running on the treadmill for a minimum of 20 minutes each day between 6:00 a.m. and 7:00 a.m.

Or …

To guarantee that I improve my grades, I am committed to blocking out multiple 4-hour time blocks during the week to focus solely on my classes and identify the areas in which I need to reach out to my professor for help.

The more specific your actions are, the clearer your programming will be so that you consistently take the actions required to move you closer to your goals. Be sure to include *frequency* (how often), *quantity* (how many), and *precise time frames* (when you will begin and end your activities).

Step Three: Recite Your Affirmations Every Morning with Emotion

Remember, your Miracle Morning affirmations aren't designed only to make you *feel good*. These written statements are strategically engineered to program your subconscious mind with the beliefs and mindset you need to achieve your desired outcomes, while directing your conscious mind to keep you focused on your highest priorities and taking the actions that will get you there.

For your affirmations to be effective, however, it is important that you tap into your emotions while reciting them. Mindlessly repeating an affirmation without intentionally feeling its truth will have minimal impact for you. You must take responsibility for generating authentic emotions such as excitement and determination, and powerfully infuse those emotions into every affirmation you recite.

You must affirm who you need to be to do the things you need to do so that you can have the results that you want. I'll say this again: It isn't magic. This strategy works when you connect with *the person you need to become* on the way to achieving your goals. It's who you are that attracts your results more than anything else.

Action: Schedule time each day to read your affirmations during your Miracle Morning to program your subconscious and focus your conscious mind on what's most important to you and what you are committed to doing to make it your reality. That's right, you must read them daily. Reading your affirmation occasionally is as effective as an occasional workout. You'll start seeing results only when you've made them a part of your daily routine.

A great place to read affirmations is in the shower. If you laminate them and leave them there, then they will be in front of you every day. Put them anywhere you can to remind you: an index card under your car's sun visor, a sticky note on your bathroom mirror—you can even write them directly on a mirror with dry-erase markers. The more you encounter them, the more the subconscious mind can connect with them to change your thinking and your actions.

Step Four: Constantly Update and Evolve Your Affirmations

As you continue to grow, improve, and evolve, so should your affirmations. When you come up with a new goal, dream, or any extraordinary result you want to create for your life, add it to your affirmations.

Personally, I have affirmations for every single significant area of my life (finances, health, happiness, relationships, profession, etc.), and I continually update them as I learn more. And I am always on the lookout for quotes, strategies, and philosophies that I can add to improve my mindset. Anytime you come across an empowering quote or philosophy and think *Wow that is an area where I could make a huge improvement*, add it to your affirmations.

Remember, your affirmations should be tailored to you, what you are *personally* committed to. They must be specific for them to work on your subconscious.

Your programming can change and improve at any time, starting right now. You can reprogram any perceived limitations with new beliefs and create new behaviors so you can become as successful as you want to be in any area of life you choose.

In summary, your new affirmations articulate the extraordinary results you are committed to creating, why they are critically important to you, and, most importantly, which necessary actions you are committed to taking, and when, to ensure that you attain and sustain the extraordinary levels of success you truly want (and deserve) for your life.

Affirmations to Become a Level 10 College Student

In addition to the formula to create your own affirmations, I have included this list of sample affirmations, which may help spark your creativity. Feel free to include any of these that resonate with you.

- I am just as worthy, deserving, and capable of achieving personal and academic success as any other person on earth, and I will prove that today with my actions.

- I am becoming healthier each day because I am committed to making healthy choices for my body and my mind every day.

- Where I *am* is a result of who I *was*, but where I go depends entirely on who I *choose to be* starting today.

- I choose to take 100% responsibility for my own success, because my success depends on my actions and decisions each day.

- I am a hardworking, intelligent student and I committed to excelling in my major and career.

- I am fully committed to dedicating 30–60 minutes to do my Miracle Morning and the Life S.A.V.E.R.S. so that I can continue to become the person I need to be to create everything I want for my life.

- I am fully committed to replace my complaints with words of gratitude, because even in the midst of difficulty, gratitude will bring more appreciation to the present moment than complaining.

- I am grateful for all my wins, and most especially for all my "losses," because each of those experiences holds knowledge about how I can further improve as a student and as an individual.

- I focus on learning new things and improving my self-awareness daily, and I commit to reading or rereading at least one book to help that effort every month.

- I continue to learn more about myself by asking myself the right questions so that I will create a clearer picture of my overall vision for myself.

- I am committed to constant and never-ending improvement in the tasks necessary for the day-to-day functioning of a college student.

These are just a few examples of affirmations. You can use any that resonate with you, but do create your own using the four-step formula described in the previous pages. Anything you repeat to yourself over and over again with emotion will be programmed in your subconscious mind, help you form new beliefs, and manifest through your actions.

"V" IS FOR VISUALIZATION

Visualization has long been a well-known practice of world-class athletes, who use it to optimize their performance. Olympic athletes and top performers in many sports incorporate visualization as a critical part of their daily training. What is less well known is that the top achievers among successful entrepreneurs use it just as frequently.

Visualization is a technique by which you use your imagination to create a compelling picture of your future, providing you with heightened clarity and producing the motivation that will assist you in making your vision a reality.

To understand *why* visualization works, you need to look at mirror neurons. A neuron is a cell that connects the brain and other parts of the body, and a mirror neuron is one that fires or sends an impulse when we take an action *or* observe someone else taking action. This is a relatively new area of study in neurology, but these cells seem to allow us to improve our abilities by watching other people perform them *or* by visualizing ourselves performing them. Some studies indicate, for example, that experienced weight lifters can increase muscle mass through vivid visualization sessions, and mirror neurons get the credit for making this possible. In many ways, the brain can't tell the difference between a vivid visualization and an actual experience.

I was always a little skeptical about the value of visualization because it sounded a little too new agey. Once I read about mirror neurons, my whole attitude changed!

What Do You Visualize?

Most people are limited by visions of their past results. They replay previous failures and heartbreaks. Creative visualization, however, enables you to *design* the vision that will occupy your mind, ensuring that the greatest pull on you is your future—a compelling, exciting, and limitless future.

Many people don't feel comfortable visualizing success and are even scared to succeed. They may experience resistance to this practice. Some may even feel guilty that they will leave colleagues, friends, and family members behind when they become successful.

This famous quote from Marianne Williamson is a great reminder for anyone who feels mental or emotional obstacles when attempting to visualize:

Our deepest fear is not that we are inadequate. Our deepest fear is that we are powerful beyond measure. It is our light, not our darkness, that most frightens us. We ask ourselves, "Who am I to be brilliant, gorgeous, talented, fabulous?" Actually, who are you not to be? You are a child of God. Your playing small does not serve the world. There is nothing enlightened about shrinking so that other people won't feel insecure around you. We are all meant to shine, as children do. We were born to make manifest the glory of God that is within us. It's not just in some of us; it's in everyone. And as we let our own light shine, we unconsciously give other people permission to do the same. As we are liberated from our own fear, our presence automatically liberates others.

Consider that the greatest gift you can give to those you love and those you lead is to live to your full potential. What does that look like for you?

After I've read my affirmations during my Miracle Morning practice, I sit upright, close my eyes, and take a few slow, deep breaths. For the next five to ten minutes, I simply visualize the *specific actions* that are necessary for my long- and short-term goals to become a reality.

Notice that I do *not* visualize the results. Many people will disagree on this, but there is scientific evidence showing that merely visualizing the result you want (e.g., the new car, the dream house, crossing the finish line, standing on stage, etc.) can actually diminish your drive because your brain has already experienced the reward on some level. Instead, I highly recommend focusing your visualization on the necessary actions. Visualize yourself performing the actions—especially those that you habitually resist and procrastinate on—in a way that creates a compelling mental and emotional experience of the action. For example, Hal despised running, but he had made a commitment to himself (and publically) to run a 52-mile ultramarathon. Throughout his five months of training, he used Miracle Morning Visualization to see himself lacing up his running shoes and hitting the pavement—*with a smile on his face and pep in his step*—so that when it was time to train, he had already programmed the experience to be positive and enjoyable.

You might picture yourself enjoying getting your work done. Spend time imagining studying for an exam, for example. What does it look like? How does it feel as you remain focused and understand the concepts? Picture yourself responding to obstacles and issues with ease.

If writing papers is a chore for you like it used to be for me, you can visualize yourself calmly outlining your paper. Imagine that you are excited to work on your paper for the freedom waiting for you after it is finished!

You can pick anything that is a critical action step or skill that you may not be performing at your best yet. Envisioning success and what it takes to get there will prepare you for, and almost ensure, a successful day.

Three Simple Steps for Miracle Morning Visualization

The perfect time to visualize yourself living in alignment with your affirmations is right after you read them.

Step One: Get Ready

Some people like to play instrumental music in the background during their visualization, such as classical or baroque (check out anything from the composer J. S. Bach). If you'd like to experiment with music, put it on with the volume relatively low. Personally, I find anything with words to be distracting.

Now, sit up tall in a comfortable position. This can be on a chair, the couch, or the floor with a cushion. Breathe deeply. Close your eyes, clear your mind, and let go of any self-imposed limitations as you prepare yourself for the benefits of visualization.

Step Two: Visualize What You Really Want

What do you really want? Forget about logic, limits, and being practical. If you could reach any heights, personally and professionally, what would that look like? See, feel, hear, touch, taste, and smell every detail of your vision. Involve all your senses to maximize effectiveness. The more vivid you make your vision, the more compelled you'll be to take the necessary actions to make it a reality.

Step Three: Visualize Yourself Taking and Enjoying the Necessary Actions

Once you've created a clear mental picture of what you want, begin to see yourself doing precisely what you need to do to achieve your vision, doing it with supreme confidence, and enjoying every step of the process. See yourself engaged in the actions you'll need to take (exercising, writing, selling, presenting, public speaking, making calls, sending emails, etc.). Imagine the look and *feeling* or supreme confidence as you study. See and *feel* yourself smiling as you're running on your treadmill filled with a sense of pride for your self-discipline to follow through on your commitment. In other words, visualize yourself doing what you must do, and thoroughly enjoying the process, especially if it's a process you don't naturally enjoy. Imagine what it would look and feel like if you did enjoy it.

Picture the look of determination on your face as you confidently and consistently get your work done, turn in that paper, take care of your health, do well on your exams, and work to improve yourself. Visualize your family, friends, and roommates responding to your positive demeanor and optimistic outlook.

Seeing yourself as the person who has it all together is the first step in actually getting it all together. Imagine yourself joyfully sitting down with your planner and organizing the upcoming days and weeks with the classes and events you need to attend, hours set aside for studying, and papers you need to complete. Visualize yourself doing it all with ease and peace, and achieving great success.

Final Thoughts on Visualization

Visualization can be a powerful aid in overcoming self-limiting beliefs as well as self-limiting habits such as procrastination, and get you consistently performing the actions necessary to achieve extraordinary results in your life. When you combine reading your affirmations every morning with daily visualization, you will turbocharge the programming of your subconscious mind for success through peak performance. Your thoughts and feelings will align with your vision so that you can maintain the motivation you need to continue to take the necessary actions and achieve academically.

"E" IS FOR EXERCISE

Exercise should be a staple of your Miracle Morning. Even a few minutes of exercise each day significantly enhances your health, improves your self-confidence and emotional well-being, and enables you to think better and concentrate longer. You'll also notice how quickly your energy increases with daily exercise, and the people you spend the most time with will notice it, too.

Personal development experts and self-made multimillionaire entrepreneurs Eben Pagan and Tony Robbins (who is also a best-selling author) both agree that the number one key to success is to start every morning with a personal success ritual. Included in both of their success rituals is some type of morning exercise. Eben is adamant about the importance of *morning* exercise: "Every morning, you've got to get your heart rate up and get your blood flowing and fill your lungs with oxygen." He continues, "Don't just exercise at the end of the day, or at the middle of the day. And even if you do like to exercise at those times, always incorporate at least 10 to 20 minutes of jumping jacks, or some sort of aerobic exercise in the morning." Hey, if it works for Eben and Tony, it works for me!

Lest you think you have to engage in triathlon or marathon training, think again. Your morning exercise also doesn't need to replace an afternoon or evening regimen if you already have one in place. You can still hit the gym at the usual time. However, the benefits from adding as little as five minutes of morning exercise are undeniable, including improved blood pressure and blood-sugar levels and decreased risk of all kinds of scary things like heart disease, osteoporosis, cancer, and diabetes. Maybe most importantly, a little exercise in the morning will increase your energy levels for the rest of the day to help you keep up with the ups and downs of life.

You can go for a walk or run, follow along to a yoga video on YouTube, or find a Life S.A.V.E.R.S. buddy and play some early morning racquetball. There's also an excellent app called 7 Minute Workout that gives you a full body workout in—you guessed it—seven minutes. The choice is yours, but pick one activity and do it.

As a college student, you are constantly on the go. You need an endless reserve of energy to make the best of the challenges that come your way, and a daily morning exercise practice is going to provide it.

Exercise for Your Brain

Even if you don't care about your physical health, consider that exercise is simply going to make you smarter, and that can only help your problem-solving abilities. Dr. Steven Masley, a Florida physician and nutritionist with a health practice geared toward executives, explains how exercise creates a direct connection to your cognitive ability.

"If we're talking about brain performance, the best predictor of brain speed is aerobic capacity—how well you can run up a hill is very strongly correlated with brain speed and cognitive shifting ability," Masley said.

Masley has designed a corporate wellness program based on the work he's done with more than 1,000 patients. "The average person going into these programs will increase brain speed by 25–30 percent."

Hal chose yoga for his exercise activity and began practicing it shortly after he created the Miracle Morning. He's been doing it and loving it ever since. My exercise routine differs.

I try to make my exercise routine as fun as possible. I made a playlist of my most favorite songs, and I literally have a dance party, because why not?! I pair that with a 1- to 2-minute plank to wake up my core, followed by some pushups and some stretching and breathing at the end of it. It is important to get your heart rate up! As someone who has a love-hate relationship with exercise, I am always proud of myself for doing those few minutes of planks and increasing my pushups each day. In the end, I just have fun! Starting my day off that way sets up each day to be the best day ever.

There are some days that I am too tired when waking up, so I also do restorative yoga. I love the workouts of an amazing trainer and friend, Andrea Riggs. She has terrific Zumba videos and also is a strong supporter of yoga. She always says, "If you can breathe, you can do yoga." Working out along with her short videos is great for your Miracle Morning practice.

Find what resonates with you, and make it a part of your Miracle Morning.

Final Thoughts on Exercise

You know that if you want to maintain good health and increase your energy, you must exercise consistently. That's not news to anyone. But what also isn't news is how easy it is to make excuses. Two of the biggest are "I don't have time" and "I'm too tired." And those are just the first two on the list. There is no limit to the excuses you can think of. And the more creative you are, the more excuses you can find!

That's the beauty of incorporating exercise into your Miracle Morning—it happens before your day wears you out and before you've had hours to come up with new excuses. Because it comes first, the Miracle Morning is a surefire way to avoid those stumbling blocks and make exercise a daily habit.

Legal disclaimer: Hopefully this goes without saying, but you should consult your physician before beginning any exercise regimen, especially if you are experiencing any physical pain, discomfort, disabilities, etc. You may need to modify or even refrain from an exercise routine to meet your individual needs.

"R" IS FOR READING

One of the fastest ways to achieve everything you want is to find successful people to be your role models. For every goal you have, there's a good chance an expert out there has already achieved the same thing or something similar. As Tony Robbins says, "Success leaves clues."

Fortunately, some of the best of the best have shared their stories in writing. And that means all those success blueprints are just waiting for anyone willing to invest the time in reading. Books are a limitless supply of help and mentorship right at your fingertips.

Occasionally, I hear somebody say, "I'm just not a big reader." I get it. I never considered myself a big reader, either. I was just better at math. In high school, I had a lot of books to read for my classes, which made the idea of reading not fun. I could not figure out how so many people could read books that were hundreds of pages long and enjoy it. On standardized tests, I did not even try doing well in the reading comprehension section. I was a slow reader, and it would take me multiple times to read something in order to understand it.

By doing my Miracle Morning, I have come to love reading. The best part is that you get to read what *you* want or need, not what is assigned for class. There is so much knowledge out there waiting to be read, and I have found that reading is one of the greatest ways to invest in yourself for your future.

Here are some of my favorite books that will specifically help you improve as a college student.

On Being a College Student

- *How to Become a Straight-A Student: The Unconventional Strategies Real College Students Use to Score High While Studying Less* by Cal Newport
- *The Last Lecture* by Randy Pausch
- *Debt-Free U* by Zac Bissonnette
- *10 Steps to Earning Awesome Grades (While Studying Less)* by Thomas Frank
- *Skating Through College: How to Pursue Your Passions and Make a Difference Without Sacrificing Your GPA* by John P Israel
- *Living College Life in the Front Row* by Jon Vroman
- *Do Your Laundry or You'll Die Alone: Advice Your Mom Would Give If She Thought You Were Listening* by Becky Blades

- *How to Win at College: Surprising Secrets for Success from the Country's Top Students* by Cal Newport
- *23 Anti-Procrastination Habits: How to Stop Being Lazy and Get Results You Want* by S. J. Scott
- *Why Didn't They Teach Me This in School?: 99 Personal Money Management Principles to Live By* by Cary Siegel
- *Born for This: How to Find the Work You Were Meant to Do* by Chris Guillebeau
- *You Are a Badass: How to Stop Doubting Your Greatness and Start Living an Awesome Life* by Jen Sincero
- *What the Best College Students Do* by Ken Bain
- *The Defining Decade: Why Your Twenties Matter—and How to Make the Most of Them Now* by Meg Jay
- *Life After College: The Complete Guide to Getting What You Want* by Jenny Blake
- *Never Pay Retail for College* by Beth W. Walker

On Mindset

- *The Art of Exceptional Living* by Jim Rohn
- *The One Thing: The Surprisingly Simple Truth Behind Extraordinary Results* by Gary Keller and Jay Papasan
- *The 7 Habits of Highly Effective People: Powerful Lessons in Personal Change* by Stephen R. Covey
- *Mastery* by Robert Greene
- *The 4-Hour Workweek: Escape 9–5, Live Anywhere, and Join the New Rich* by Tim Ferriss
- *The Game of Life and How to Play It* by Florence Scovel Shinn
- *The Compound Effect* by Darren Hardy
- *Man's Search for Meaning* by Viktor Frankl

- *Taking Life Head On: How to Love the Life You Have While You Create the Life of Your Dreams* by Hal Elrod
- *Think and Grow Rich* by Napoleon Hill
- *Vision to Reality: How Short Term Massive Action Equals Long Term Maximum Results* by Honorée Corder
- *Finding Your Element: How to Discover Your Talents and Passions and Transform Your Life* by Sir Ken Robinson and Lou Aronica

In addition to finding confidence as a student, you can transform your relationships, increase your self-esteem, improve your communication skills, learn how to become healthy, and improve any other area of your life you can think of. Head to your library or local bookstore—or do what I do and visit Amazon.com—and you'll find more books than you can possibly imagine on any area of your life you want to improve.

For a complete list of Hal's favorite personal development books—including those that have made the biggest impact on his success and happiness—check out the Recommended Reading list at TMMBook.com.

How Much Should You Read?

I recommend making a commitment to read a minimum of ten pages per day (although five is okay to start with if you read slowly or don't yet enjoy reading).

Ten pages may not seem like a lot, but let's do the math. Reading ten pages a day adds up to 3,650 pages per year, which stacks up to approximately eighteen 200-page books that will enable you to take yourself to the next level so that you can take your success in your academic and professional life to the next level. All in just 10–15 minutes of daily reading, or 15–30 minutes if you read more slowly.

Let me ask you, if you read eighteen personal and professional development books in the next twelve months, do you think you'll improve your mindset, gain more confidence, and learn proven strategies that will accelerate your success? Do you think you'll be a better, more capable version of who you are today? Do you think that will be reflected in your results? Absolutely! Reading ten pages per day is not going to break you, but it will absolutely make you.

Final Thoughts on Reading

- Begin with the end in mind by considering this question: What do you hope to gain from the book? Take a moment to do this now by asking yourself what you want to gain from reading this one.

- Books don't have to be read cover to cover, nor do they have to be finished. Remember that this is *your* reading time. Use the table of contents to make sure you read the parts you care about most, and don't hesitate to put it down and move to another book if you aren't enjoying it or gaining value from it. You have too many options for incredible information to spend time on the mediocre.

- Many Miracle Morning practitioners use their reading time to catch up on their religious texts, such as the Bible, Torah, Quran, and others.

- Unless you're borrowing a book from the library or a friend, feel free to underline, circle, highlight, dog-ear, and take notes in the margins of the book. The process of marking books as you read allows you to come back at any time and recapture the key lessons, ideas, and benefits without needing to read the book again. If you use a digital reader, such as Kindle, Nook, or an iBooks app, notes and highlighting are easily organized, so you can see them each time you flip through the book, or you can go directly to a list of your notes and highlights.

- Summarize key ideas, insights, and memorable passages in a journal. You can build your own summary of your favorite books so you can revisit the key content anytime in just minutes.

- Rereading good personal development books is an underused yet very effective strategy. Rarely can you read a book once and internalize all its value. Achieving mastery in any area requires repetition. I've read *The Miracle Morning* many times in the last three years. Each time I read it, I found the piece of information I needed to help me get to the next level. Why not try it out with this book? Commit to rereading *The Miracle Morning for College Students* as soon as you're finished to deepen your learning and give yourself more time to master the practices.

- Audiobooks count as reading! You still get the information, and you can do it while exercising or during your commute. Audiobooks are great when I have things to do that need to get done, such as cleaning my room or laundry, or even while walking between classes. That way, whatever I am doing, I still have the opportunity to learn and grow! Also, if you want to study a book carefully, listen to the audio while reading the text. It is a great way to internalize the strategies that are in the book. Audible and Overdrive are both great apps for audiobooks. On Audible, you have to pay for your audiobooks, but with Overdrive, you can link it to your local public library and check out books for free.

- Most importantly, quickly implement what you read. Schedule time to implement action steps based on advice you want to implement *while you're reading it.* Keep your calendar next to you and schedule time blocks to put the content into action. Don't become a personal development junkie who reads a lot but does very little. I've met many people who take pride in the number of books they read, as if it's some badge of honor. I'd rather read and implement one good book than read 10 books and do nothing other than start reading the 11th book. While reading is a great way to gain knowledge, insights, and strategies, it is the application and practice of what you learn that will advance your life and academics.

Are you committed to using what you're learning in this book by taking action and following through with the 30-Day Miracle Morning Challenge at the end? Glad to hear it. Let's get to the final *S* of the S.A.V.E.R.S.

"S" IS FOR SCRIBING

Scribing is simply another word for writing. Let's keep it real— Hal needed an *S* for the end of S.A.V.E.R.S. because a *W* wouldn't fit anywhere. Thanks thesaurus, we owe you one.

The scribing element of your Miracle Morning enables you to write down what you're grateful for, as well as document your insights, ideas, breakthroughs, realizations, successes, and lessons learned, including any areas of opportunity, personal growth, or improvement.

Most Miracle Morning practitioners scribe in a journal for five to ten minutes during their Miracle Morning. By getting your thoughts out of your head and putting them in writing, you'll immediately gain heightened awareness, clarity, and valuable insights that you'd otherwise forget or be oblivious to.

If you're like Hal used to be, you probably have at least a few half-used and barely touched journals and notebooks. It wasn't until he started his Miracle Morning practice that scribing quickly became one of his favorite daily habits.

Writing will give you the daily benefits of consciously directing your thoughts, but what's even more powerful are the insights you'll gain from reviewing your journals, from cover to cover, afterwards— especially at the end of the year. As Tony Robbins has said many times, "A life worth living is a life worth recording."

It is hard to put into words how overwhelmingly constructive the experience of going back and reviewing your journals can be. Michael Maher, *The Miracle Morning for Real Estate Agents* coauthor, is an avid practitioner of the Life S.A.V.E.R.S. Part of Michael's morning routine is to record his appreciations and affirmations in what he calls his Blessings Book. Michael says it best:

"What you appreciate ... APPRECIATES. It is time to take our insatiable appetite for what we want and replace it with an insatiable appetite and gratitude for what we do have. Write your appreciations, be grateful and appreciative, and you will have more of those things you crave—better relationships, more material goods, more happiness."

There is strength in writing down what you appreciate, and reviewing this material can change your mindset on a challenging day. A great practice to add to your routine is to write what you appreciate about your life at this very moment. When we write down the things we appreciate about being a student, even (and particularly) when we feel less than wonderful about how school has been going, it's easier to focus on the positive aspects or qualities.

For example, you may be angry about an exam you did not do well because you did not have enough time to study, but afterwards you have the power to use this as a learning experience rather than remaining angry about it. Instead of focusing on the negative part, be grateful that you have room to grow, and you can find out exactly what to do to improve! Another example would be when your professor decides to add something to an assignment the night before it is due. It would be easy to get frustrated, but instead you can feel grateful that you are having another opportunity to learn and challenge your mind. The practice of recording those appreciations helps you focus on the positive, which will help you stay flexible and solution-focused even when circumstances are challenging.

While many worthwhile benefits flow from keeping a daily journal, here are a few of my favorites. With daily scribing, you'll ...

- **Gain Clarity**—Journaling will give you more clarity and understanding of your past and current circumstances, help you work through present challenges you're facing, and allow you to brainstorm, prioritize, and plan your actions each day to optimize your future.

- **Capture Ideas**—You will be able to capture, organize, and expand on your ideas and keep from losing the important ones that you are saving for an opportune moment in the future.

- **Review Lessons**—Journaling provides a place to record, reference, and review all of the lessons you're learning, both from your wins and any mistakes you make along the way.

- **Acknowledge Your Progress**—Rereading your journal entries from a year or even a week ago and observing how much progress you've made can be hugely beneficial. We often accomplish a task or goal and move on to the next without appreciating our efforts. Noticing how far you've come truly is one of the most enjoyable, eye-opening, and confidence-inspiring experiences, and it can't be duplicated any other way.

- **Improve Your Memory**—People tend to assume they will remember things, but if you've ever gone to the grocery store without a list, you know this is simply untrue. When we write something down, we are much more likely to remember it, and if we forget, we can always go back and read it again.

Effective Journaling

Here are three simple steps to get started with journaling or improve your current journaling process.

1. Choose a format: physical or digital.

You'll want to decide up front if you prefer a traditional, physical journal or a digital journal (on your computer or an app for your mobile device). If you aren't sure, experiment with both and see which feels best.

2. Obtain the journal of your choice.

Almost anything can work, but when it comes to a physical journal, there is something to be said for a durable one that you enjoy looking at—after all, ideally you're going to have it for the rest of your life. I like to buy high quality leather journals with lines on the pages, but it's your journal, so choose what works best for you. Some people prefer journals without lines so they can draw or create mind maps. Others like to have a predated book with a page for each day of the year to help them stay accountable.

Here are a few favorite physical journals from The Miracle Morning Facebook Community:

- *The Miracle Morning Companion Planner* is your hands-on guide for building a happier and more fulfilling life and career. This 12-month, undated planner allows you to start at any time of the year! Incorporating and tracking the Life S.A.V.E.R.S. each day will help you to be more present and intentional in each moment, own every aspect of your day, and to get the most out of your life. Check out a free preview here: MiracleMorning.com/PlannerSample.

- *The Five Minute Journal* has become popular among top performers. It has a very specific format for each day with prompts, such as "I am grateful for …" and "What would make today great?" It takes five minutes or less and includes an evening option so you can review your day. (FiveMinuteJournal.com)

- *The Freedom Journal* gives you a structured daily process that is focused on helping you with a single objective: *Accomplish Your #1 Goal in 100 Days*. Beautifully designed by John Lee Dumas of Entrepreneur On Fire, it's meant specifically to help you set and accomplish one big goal at a time. (TheFreedomJournal.com)

- *The Plan: Your Legendary Life Planner* was designed by friends of mine, Brandy Salazar and Matt Aitchison, and it is a goal-setting and habit-tracking system and planner for people who are ready for life balance and are willing to be intentional about achieving Level 10 in all areas of life. (LegendaryLifePlan.com)

- *The Miracle Morning Journal* is designed specifically to enhance and support your Miracle Morning and to keep you organized and accountable and to track your S.A.V.E.R.S.

each day. You can also download a free sample of *The Miracle Morning Journal* today at TMMbook.com to make sure it's right for you. (MiracleMorningJournal.com)

If you prefer to use a digital journal, many choices are available. Here are a few favorites:

- *Five Minute Journal* also offers an iPhone app, which follows the same format as the physical version, but allows you to upload photographs to your daily entries, and also sends you helpful reminders to input your entries each morning and evening. (FiveMinuteJournal.com)

- *Day One* is a popular journaling app, and it's perfect if you don't want any structure or any limits on how much you can write. Day One offers a blank page for each daily entry, so if you like to write lengthy journal entries, this may be the app for you. (DayOneApp.com)

- *Penzu* is a popular online journal, which doesn't require an iPhone, iPad, or Android device. All you need is a computer. (Penzu.com)

Again, it really comes down to your preference and the features you want. If none of these digital options resonates with you, type "online journal" into Google, or simply type "journal" into the app store, and you'll get a variety of choices.

3. Scribe daily.

You'll find endless things you can write about—notes from the book you're reading, a list of things you're grateful for, and your top three to five priorities for the day are good items to start with. Write whatever makes you feel good and helps you optimize your day. Don't worry about grammar, spelling, or punctuation. Your journal is a place to let your imagination run wild, so keep a muzzle on your inner critic and don't edit—just scribe!

CUSTOMIZING YOUR S.A.V.E.R.S.

I know that you might have days when you can't do the Miracle Morning practice all at once. Feel free to split up the Life S.A.V.E.R.S. in any way that works for you. Here is an example. There are some days that you slept through your alarm, needed to get to class, and missed your morning time. We're only human; it happens to the best of us, most especially as college students! Take the rest of the day as an opportunity to complete the Life S.A.V.E.R.S. anyway. Try to do short meditations before each class. Write an affirmation down and repeat it to yourself. Visualize yourself going through your busy day with ease, confidence, and success. You are already exercising as you are sprinting from one class to another. Your "reading" is the knowledge you are gaining from your professor. Lastly, you can journal in the Notes app on your phone before your bedtime. Just be sure to tell yourself at least one affirmation and visualize going through your busy day with ease, confidence, and success.

I want to share a few ideas specifically geared toward customizing the Life S.A.V.E.R.S. based on your schedule and preferences. Your current morning routine might allow you to fit in only a 6-, 20-, or 30-minute Miracle Morning, or you might choose to do a longer version on the weekends.

Here is an example of a fairly common 60-minute Miracle Morning schedule using the Life S.A.V.E.R.S.

Silence: 10 minutes

Affirmations: 5 minutes

Visualization: 5 minutes

Exercise: 10 minutes

Reading: 20 minutes

Scribing: 10 minutes

You can customize the sequence, too. Before even beginning, I make sure I keep my phone on airplane mode. There is no email,

Facebook notification, or text message that is as important as your Miracle Morning routine, a time that you have set aside for you! I do not even turn on my laptop because I associate it with doing homework, which does not help me remain present for my Miracle Morning routine. I begin with exercise to get my heart pumping and the oxygen flowing to my brain. Then I meditate, which helps me center myself. Clear-minded, I read my affirmations. Then I visualize what I need to do for the day, my short-term goals, and my long-term goals. After that, I read at least 10 pages of the book I am currently reading. Lastly, I scribe about whatever I am grateful for, the next steps I need to take to accomplish my goals, and the intention(s) that I want to set for that day. Hal prefers to start with a period of peaceful, purposeful Silence so that he can wake up slowly, clear his mind, and focus his energy and intentions. However, this is your Miracle Morning, not ours—feel free to experiment with different sequences to see which you like best.

There were some days in college when I had to spread the Life S.A.V.E.R.S. throughout my day. If I had an early exam that day, I started my day with meditation to calm my mind and switched out my Reading for studying time so that I could review some of my notes before the exam. Right before the exam, I would write down on a sheet of paper an affirmation that could put me in the right mindset before taking the exam, and visualize answering each question fully and accurately. This usually helped me stay calm, which helped me do better on my exams. After taking the exam, I would take my next free chance to read at least 10 pages in the book I was reading and go for a 20-minute run.

EGO DEPLETION AND YOUR MIRACLE MORNING

Have you ever wondered why you can resist sugary snacks in the morning, but your resistance crumbles in the afternoon or evening? Why is it that sometimes willpower is strong and other times it deserts us? It turns out that willpower is like a muscle that grows tired from use, and by the end of the day it is harder to push ourselves to do activities that serve us and avoid those that don't.

The good news is that we know how this works and can set ourselves up for success with some advance planning. And the great news? The Miracle Morning is an integral part of your plan. To see how this works, we need to understand ego depletion.

Ego depletion is a term to describe "a person's diminished capacity to regulate their thoughts, feelings, and actions," according to Roy F. Baumeister and John Tierney, the authors of *Willpower: Rediscovering the Greatest Human Strength.* Ego depletion grows worse at the end of the day and when we are hungry, tired, or have had to exert our willpower too often or for long durations.

If you wait until the end of the day to do important things that give you energy and help you become the person and student you want to be, you'll find that your excuses are more compelling and your motivation has gone missing. But when you wake up and do your Miracle Morning first thing, you gain the increased energy and mindfulness that the Life S.A.V.E.R.S. provide and keep ego depletion from getting in your way.

When you perform the Life S.A.V.E.R.S. habit every day, you learn the mechanics of habit formation when your willpower is strongest, and you can use this knowledge and energy to adopt small and doable habits at other times of the day.

FINAL THOUGHTS ON THE LIFE S.A.V.E.R.S.

Everything is difficult before it's easy. Every new experience is uncomfortable before it's comfortable. The more you practice the Life S.A.V.E.R.S., the more natural and normal each of them will feel. Hal's first time meditating was almost his last because his mind raced like a Ferrari, and his thoughts bounced around uncontrollably like the silver sphere in a pinball machine. Now he loves meditation, and while he's still no master, he says he's decent at it.

Similarly, I had trouble with visualization when I first started my Miracle Mornings. As a student, I did not really know what I wanted to become, so it was difficult for me to visualize what I was working towards. Over time, I understood that visualization was not about focusing on the final product, but instead on seeing yourself overcome the obstacles that you will face. Even though I did not know what I wanted to do with my major and all the other questions I did not have an answer to, I began visualizing myself overcoming academic obstacles like procrastination, fear, and anxiety. I also visualized myself focused while studying for exams in the hopes that I would do well. My goal was always to excel in my academics. These were my short-term visualizations. I also had visualizations for my long-term goal of walking across the graduation stage. Everything I do in my life is for my family, and I wanted my parents, brother, aunts and uncles, and all of my cousins, older and younger, to see me walk across the graduation stage. The details that I used to visualize my short-term and long-term goals gave my mind a picture of what I was going to manifest in my life.

In fact, during my senior year, I knew that the one thing I wanted to do after graduating was to write this book. I visualized myself writing *The Miracle Morning for College Students* even before I reached out to Hal. That visualization opened my mind to the steps I could take to create that opportunity for myself and become the coauthor. What I have found is that if you can visualize something, then you can do it. Visualization is a very powerful tool, so even if it uncomfortable when you start doing it, customize it to your goals and dreams and it will start working for you!

I invite you to begin practicing the Life S.A.V.E.R.S. now, so you can become familiar and comfortable with each of them and get a jump-start before you begin The 30-Day Miracle Morning Challenge in chapter 11.

THE SIX-MINUTE MIRACLE MORNING

If your biggest concern is finding time, don't worry. I've got you covered. You can actually do the entire Miracle Morning—receiving the full benefits of all six S.A.V.E.R.S.—in only six minutes a day. While six minutes isn't the duration I'd recommend on a daily basis, for those days when you're pressed for time, simply do each of the S.A.V.E.R.S. for one minute each:

Minute One (S): Close your eyes and enjoy a moment of peaceful, purposeful silence to clear your mind and get centered for your day.

Minute Two (A): Read your most important affirmation to reinforce *what* result you want to accomplish, *why* it's important to you, *which* specific actions you must take, and, most importantly, precisely *when* you will commit to taking those actions

Minute Three (V): Visualize yourself flawlessly executing the single most important action that you want to mentally rehearse for the day.

Minute Four (E): Stand up and engage in some high energy jumping jacks or drop and do push-ups and crunches to get your heart rate up and engage your body.

Minute Five (R): Grab the book you're reading and read a page or paragraph.

Minute Six (S): Grab your journal and jot down one thing that you're grateful for and the single most important result for you to generate that day.

I'm sure you can see how, even in six minutes, the S.A.V.E.R.S. will set you on the right path for the day—and you can always devote more time later when your schedule permits or the opportunity presents itself. Doing the six-minute practice is a way to start a mini-habit to build your confidence or a way to bookmark the habit on a tough morning. Another mini-habit you could do is to start with one of the Life S.A.V.E.R.S., and once you get used to waking up earlier, add more of them. Remember that the objective is to have some time to work on your personal goals and mindset, so if you are overwhelmed, it's not going to work for you.

Personally, my Miracle Morning has grown into a daily ritual of renewal and inspiration that I absolutely love! In the coming chapters, I will build on the benefits of the Life S.A.V.E.R.S. and cover *a lot* of information that has the potential to turn you into a truly confident student. I can't wait to share it with you.

SECTION II:

THE NOT-SO-OBVIOUS COLLEGE STUDENT SUCCESS PRINCIPLES

Not-So-Obvious College Student Success Principle #1:

SELF-LEADERSHIP

Your level of success will seldom exceed your level of personal development ... because success is something you attract by the person you become.

—JIM ROHN

W e've been lied to. Yep. Society has conditioned all of us to think that the only way to *have* more is to *do* more.

Want better grades? Work harder. Put in *more* hours.

Want better health? Lift *more* weights and log *more* steps on your fitness tracker.

Want more love? Do *more* for your partner than they do for you.

But what if the real secret to having more of what we want in our lives is not about *doing* more, but about *becoming* more?

It is this philosophy that gave birth to, and remains the foundation of, the Miracle Morning: Our level of success *in every single area of our lives* is always determined by our levels of *personal development* (i.e., our beliefs, knowledge, emotional intelligence, skills, abilities, faith, etc.). So if we want to have more, we must first become more.

Think of it this way: If you were to measure your desired level of success on a scale of one to ten in every area of your life, it's safe to say that you want "Level 10" success in each area. I've never met anyone who said, "Nah, I don't want to be too happy, too healthy, or too successful. I am content settling for less than my potential and cruising along with a level 5 life."

But what are we doing each day to become a Level 10 person?

In other words, who you're becoming is far more important than what you're doing, and yet the irony is that what you're doing each day is determining who you're becoming.

Andrew Bryant, founder of Self-Leadership International, summed it up this way: "Self-leadership is the practice of intentionally influencing your thinking, feeling, and behaviors to achieve your objective(s) … [It] is having a developed sense of who you are, what you can do, and where you are going coupled with the ability to influence your communication, emotions, and behaviors on the way to getting there."

Before I reveal the key principles of self-leadership, I want to share with you what I've discovered about the crucial role that *mindset* plays as the foundation of effective self-leadership. Your past beliefs, self-image, and the ability to collaborate with and rely upon others at critical times will factor into your ability to excel as a self-leader.

BE AWARE—AND SKEPTICAL—OF YOUR SELF-IMPOSED LIMITATIONS

You may be holding on to false limiting beliefs that are unconsciously interfering with your ability to achieve your personal and professional goals.

For example, you may be someone who repeats "I wish I were more organized." Yet in reality, you are more than capable of providing the structure and inspiration to be organized. Thinking of yourself as less than capable assumes imminent failure and simultaneously thwarts your ability to succeed. Life contains enough obstacles without creating more for yourself!

Effective self-leaders closely examine their beliefs, decide which ones serve them, and eliminate the ones that don't.

When you find yourself thinking or saying anything that sounds like a limiting belief, from "I don't have enough time" to "I could never do that," pause and turn your self-limiting statements into empowering questions: *Where can I find more time in my schedule? How might I be able to do that?*

Doing this allows you to tap into your innate creativity and find solutions. You can always find a way when you're committed. As tennis star Martina Navratilova said, "The difference between involvement and commitment is like ham and eggs. The chicken is involved; the pig is committed." Being all-in is the key to making anything happen.

SEE YOURSELF AS BETTER THAN YOU'VE EVER BEEN

As Hal wrote in *The Miracle Morning*, most of us suffer from Rearview Mirror Syndrome, limiting our current and future results based on who we were in the past. Remember that, although *where you are is a result of who you were, where you go depends entirely on the person you choose to be from this moment forward.* This is especially important as a student. You will make mistakes. Don't let your sense of guilt about that keep you from looking forward. Learn from your mistakes, and do better next time.

I watched an interview with Sara Blakely, the founder of Spanx, who is the youngest self-made female billionaire in the United States. She attributes her success to a mindset her father instilled in her. "When I was growing up, he encouraged us to fail. We'd come home from school, and at dinner he'd say: 'What did you fail at today?' And if there was nothing, he'd be disappointed. It was a really interesting kind of reverse psychology. I would come home and say that I tried out for something, and I was just horrible, and he high-fived me." If we allow them to be, our mistakes can turn into our greatest lessons.

We all make mistakes! As human beings, we do not come with instruction manuals, and there will always be someone with an unsolicited opinion about the way you are living your life. Don't listen to the static! Be confident in your choices, and when you aren't sure, find the answers and support you need.

All successful people, at some point, made the choice to see themselves as better than they had ever been before. They stopped maintaining limiting beliefs based on their past and instead started forming beliefs based on their unlimited potential.

One of the best ways to do this is to follow the four-step Miracle Morning Affirmations formula for creating results-oriented affirmations that was outlined in the last chapter. Be sure to create affirmations that reinforce what's possible for you by reminding you of the ideal outcome, why it's important to you, which actions you're committed to taking to achieve it, and precisely when you're committed to taking those actions.

ACTIVELY SEEK SUPPORT

Seeking support is crucial for college students, yet many students struggle, suffering in silence because they assume everyone else has greater capabilities, and they often refuse to seek help.

People who are self-leaders know they can't do it alone. You might need moral support, for example, so you can replenish the energy stores that life is so famous for depleting. Or you may need accountability support to overcome your tendency to disengage when the going gets tough. We all need support in different areas of our lives, and great self-leaders understand that and use it to their benefit.

The Miracle Morning Community on Facebook is a great place to start looking for support. The members are positive and responsive. You could also try joining a local group for people with similar goals and interests. Meetup.com is a great place to find like-minded folks who are close by. I highly recommend getting an accountability partner and, if you can, a life or business coach to help you.

THE FIVE FOUNDATIONAL PRINCIPLES OF SELF-LEADERSHIP

Self-leadership is a skill, and all skills are built on a foundation of principles. To grow and reach the levels of success you aspire to reach, you'll need to become a proficient self-leader. My favorite way to cut the learning curve in half and decrease the time it takes to reach the top 1 percent is to adapt the principles, traits, and behaviors of those who have come before me for my own circumstances.

During Hal's twenty-five years coaching franchisees and entrepreneurs, he's seen many leaders and a myriad of effective strategies. Here are the five principles he believes will make the biggest impact on your commitment to self-leadership:

1. Take 100 Percent Responsibility

2. Prioritize Fitness and Make Exercise Enjoyable

3. Aim for Financial Freedom

4. Systematize Your World

5. Commit to Your Result-Producing Process

Principle #1: Take 100 Percent Responsibility

Here's the hard truth: If your life and academics are not where you want them to be, it's all on you.

The sooner you take ownership of that fact, the sooner you'll begin to move forward. This isn't meant to be harsh. Successful people are rarely victims. In fact, one of the reasons they are successful is that they take absolute, total, and complete responsibility for each and every aspect of their lives—whether it's personal or professional, good or bad, their job or someone else's.

While victims habitually waste their time and energy blaming others and complaining, achievers are busy creating the results and circumstances they want for their lives. While students who struggle complain that they are not doing well academically because their professors do not teach them anything in class or that they assign too much work, successful students have taken 100 percent responsibility for doing well in the class, whether that means attending more of their professor's office hours, getting a study group together, or spending more time studying and completing the work.

I heard Hal articulate a profound distinction during one of his keynote speeches: "The moment you take 100 percent responsibility for everything in your life is the same moment you claim your power to change anything in your life. However, the crucial distinction is to realize that taking responsibility is not the same thing as accepting *blame*. While blame determines who is at fault for something, responsibility determines who is committed to improving a situation. It rarely matters who is at fault. All that matters is that *you* are committed to improving your situation." He's right. And it's so empowering when you truly start to think and act accordingly. Suddenly, your life and your results are within your control.

When you take true ownership of your life, there's no time for discussing whose fault something is or who gets the blame. Playing the blame game is easy, but there's no place for it in your life. Finding reasons for why you didn't meet your goals is for the other guy, not you. You own your results—good and bad. You can celebrate the good and learn from the so-called bad. Either way, you always have a choice about how you respond or react in any and every situation.

One of the reasons this mindset is so important is that you are leading by example. If you're always looking for someone to the blame, your roommate and classmates see that, and they likely don't respect it. Like parents trying to bring out the best in their kids, remember that the people around you are always watching you, and it's crucial to live by the values that you want to bring out in them.

Here's the psychological shift I suggest you make: Take ownership and stewardship over all of your decisions, actions, and outcomes, starting right now. Replace unnecessary blame with unwavering responsibility. Even if someone else drops that ball, ask what you could have done, and more importantly what you can do in the future, to prevent that ball from being dropped. While you can't change what's in the past, the good news is that you can change everything else.

From now on, there's no doubt about who is at the wheel and who is responsible for all of your results. You make the calls, do the follow-up, decide the outcomes you want, and you get them. Your results are 100 percent your responsibility. Right?

Remember you are in the position of power, you are in control, and there are no limits to what you can accomplish.

Principle #2: Prioritize Fitness and Make Exercise Enjoyable

On a scale of one to ten, where would you rank your health and fitness? Are you fit? Strong? Do you *feel* good more often than not?

How about your energy level throughout the day? Do you have more energy than you know what to do with? Can you wake up before your alarm and do what's important, handle all the demands of the day, and put out the inevitable fires, all without struggling to make it through the day feeling exhausted and out of breath?

I covered exercise as the *E* in S.A.V.E.R.S., and yes, I'm going to discuss it again right now. It's a fact that the state of your health and fitness is a huge factor in your energy and success levels—especially for college students. You're not graded based on the times you clock in and out of the library. You're graded based on the quality of the work you produce within the time that you work. Being a college student is truly an energy sport. Like any sport, you need an extraordinary supply of energy and stamina.

It's no surprise, then, that three priorities of top performers are the quality of what they eat, their sleep, and their exercise, and you need to master each of these. I'll delve deeper into each in the next chapter on Energy Engineering, but let's start with making sure you get your daily exercise in, and the key to that is to find physical activities you actually enjoy doing.

Make exercise enjoyable. The correlations among physical fitness, happiness, and success are undeniable. It is no coincidence that you rarely see top performers who are terribly out of shape. Most schedule and invest 30–60 minutes of their time each day to hit the gym or the running trail because they understand the important role that daily exercise plays in their success.

While the *E* in S.A.V.E.R.S. ensures that you're going to start each day with 5–10 minutes of exercise, I recommended that you make a commitment to engage in additional 30–60 minute workouts at least three to five times per week. Doing so will make certain that your fitness level supports the energy and confidence you need to succeed.

Even better is to engage in some form of exercise that brings you a deep level of enjoyment. That could mean going for a hike in nature, playing Ultimate Frisbee, or getting an exercise bike and putting it in front of your TV so you can enjoy your favorite episode of *Breaking Bad* and forget that you're exercising. Or do what Hal does: He loves wakeboarding and playing basketball—two excellent forms of exercise—so he does one of them every workday. You'll actually get to see my own college-student version of Hal's foundational schedule in the coming pages so you'll know how those activities fit with the rest of his priorities.

What physical activities do you enjoy that you can commit to schedule as part of your daily exercise ritual?

Principle #3: Aim for Financial Freedom

While you are busy with studying, hanging out with your friends, and taking care of your health, it can be very easy to brush financial knowledge off to the side. Our parents learned the practical information about money while they were growing up, but lots of college students never learn how to properly handle money. It is important to learn the basics of money management and take the time to build these habits for your future. Many college students graduate with student loans, and when it comes to paying back those loans, you will thank yourself later for building these habits early in your life. Here's the advice given in an article in *U.S. News* titled "6 Must-Follow Money Tips for College Students":

1. Create a Budget.

Calculate how much money you have coming in, such as your savings, work paycheck, or from your parents, and then subtract from that figure your estimated monthly expenses. You are going to spend money on food outside of your meal plan (if you choose to have a meal plan), books, laundry, and other things you may need. This will give you an idea on how much you can save per month, which will help you later when you really need to spend money or pay back student loans. Mint.com is a really great resource for budgeting; I would definitely recommend you check that out.

2. Separate Wants from Needs.

In order to build wealth, the first step is to live below your means. How much money do you need to spend to buy food? Do you *need* to go to three concerts this month? I found myself going to a lot of concerts my freshman year of college, and it was only after attending all those concerts that I realized I had no money left for the following few months of school. It is more than okay to treat yourself here and there, but if you always treat yourself then you won't be able to use that money for things you really need.

3. Set up a Checking Account.

There are many reasons you should set up a checking account. You can carry around a debit card, which is easy to pay with, but it is also good for withdrawing money from ATMs when you do need cash. A lot of jobs now have the choice to have your paycheck sent by direct deposit so that you will have your money in your checking account without having to go to the bank and deposit it yourself. Having a checking account also creates accountability and responsibility for you to take care of your money, a skill which you will carry with you through your life.

4. Use, Don't Abuse Credit Cards.

It is great to have a credit card during college. It can help build your credit, which will be important later in life when you want to lease an apartment or buy a car. The higher your credit score, the better value you will get on these kinds of purchases. A lot of credit card companies feed off of students who do not understand the value of money or how to responsibly use a credit card. Make sure that if you are going to use a credit card during college, do it for small purchases, like lunches or cheap Uber or Lyft rides. That way, you know you will be able to pay your credit card bill the following month, and you won't add up any credit card debt, which is the very last thing you want to have as a student!

5.   Do Your Homework on Loans and Financial Aid.

A lot of students (including myself) take on student debt without understanding how much debt they will have by graduation, or how they're going to be able to pay for it after graduating college. Find out how much debt you are accumulating over the years and then create a plan for how you are going to pay it back. If you grow in the awareness of the debt you have, you can create an appropriate plan to pay it all off. Find out what scholarships your school offers and whether you are eligible to apply.

6.   Shop Smart for Textbooks.

This was an area of victory for me when I began college. When I first saw how expensive books were for college classes, I knew there had to be a place where I could buy the same books at cheaper prices. After lots of research, I found DealOz.com, which is an amazing price-comparison website where you can find the cheapest prices for your books in whatever condition you want: new, used, or rental. The website sometimes has additional coupons you can use to knock more dollars off your purchase, so you are always getting the best deal possible. Over time, you can save so much money just by using this website to compare book prices.

Sometimes, professors do not even use the book(s) they ask you to buy. Make sure to email your professor and ask them how much you will use the book for the class. They are usually very honest about it, and they will tell you if you are going to need the book or not need it at all. There were some classes I had to buy five books for and we used all of them in class, but then there were other classes where I only had to buy one book that we did not use at all. It all depends on the type of class and the professor. Talking to your professor about this can save you hundreds of dollars per semester, so shop smart!

These positive habits you create for yourself will be beneficial for you on your journey toward financial freedom.

In whatever path you take after college, you will need money to survive. I encourage you to take 100 percent responsibility for your financial situation.

As college students or recent college graduates, the best time to start saving a percentage of your income is right now. Whether you're 20, 40, 60, or 80 years old, it's never too late to take control of your personal finances. You'll find an incredible boost in energy from taking charge, and you'll be able to use your accumulated savings to create even more wealth because you'll actually have money to invest in new opportunities. Sounds good, right?

People often focus on learning how to make more money, but it turns out that this is only half the battle. Learning how to *keep* it by saving and investing wisely is the second part of the puzzle.

Financial freedom isn't something you achieve overnight. It is a result of developing the mindset and habits *now* that will take you down the path that leads to financial freedom. Here are several practical steps you can start taking today to ensure that you are aiming your financial habits toward a future of financial freedom.

1. Set aside 10 percent of your income to save and invest.

This is a must. In fact, I recommend that you start by taking 10 percent of whatever funds you have in the bank right now and putting it into a separate savings account. (Go ahead. I'll wait.) Make whatever adjustments you need to make to your lifestyle to live off 90 percent of your current income. A little discipline and sacrifice goes a long way. As you see that 10 percent add up over time, it gets exciting, and you'll start to feel what's possible for the future.

2. Take another 10 percent and give it away.

Most wealthy people give a percentage of their income to causes they believe in. But you don't have to wait until you're wealthy to start this practice. Tony Robbins said, "If you won't give $1 out of $10, you'll never give $1 million out of $10 million." Can't do 10 percent or the rent check will bounce? Fine, start with 5, 2, or 1 percent. It's not the amount that matters, but developing the mindset and creating the habit that will change your financial future and serve you for the rest of your life. You've got to start teaching your subconscious brain that it can produce an abundant income, there's more than enough, and more is always on the way.

3. Continuously develop your money mindset.

It's one of the most important topics for you to master, and you can start by adding the following books, which cover various aspects of financial freedom, to your reading list:

- *Think and Grow Rich* by Napoleon Hill
- *The Richest Man in Babylon* by George Samuel Clason
- *Rich Dad Poor Dad* by Robert Kiyosaki
- *Secrets of the Millionaire Mind: Mastering the Inner Game of Wealth* by T. Harv Ecker
- *The Total Money Makeover: A Proven Plan for Financial Fitness* by Dave Ramsey
- *The Millionaire Fastlane: Crack the Code to Wealth and Live Rich for a Lifetime* by MJ DeMarco
- *Profit First: A Simple System to Transform Any Business from a Cash-Eating Monster to a Money-Making Machine* by Mike Michalowicz
- *MONEY: Master the Game: 7 Simple Steps to Financial Freedom* by Tony Robbins

4. Diversify Your Sources of Income.

Although this information may seem outside of your college student responsibilities, it is important for you to be introduced to it now for your own financial knowledge. Whether you become a serial entrepreneur, a teacher, a writer, an independent contractor, or a CEO, or you work a 9-to-5 job after graduating college, you will understand the value of financial security in the present and will sense the desire for financial freedom in the as-soon-as-possible future. Creating one or more additional streams of income is no longer a luxury. In today's unpredictable economy, it has become a necessity, and something I learned only after graduating college.

Diversifying your sources of income, also known as creating multiple streams of income, is one of the best decisions you can make. It is not only crucial to protect yourself from the unavoidable ups and downs of economic cycles, but also to establish a lifetime of financial independence. Due to the financial risks that come from relying on one source of income, such as a job or even a business, I highly recommend beginning to focus on creating at least one or more additional sources to generate cash flow.

Your additional income streams can be active, passive, or a combination of the two. Some may pay you for doing work that you love (active), while others can provide income for you without your having to do much of anything at all (passive). You can diversify your income streams among different industries to protect you against major losses during downturns in one market and allow you to financially benefit from the upswings in another.

At 25, Hal began planning his exit strategy to leave a hall-of-fame sales career to pursue his dream of becoming a full-time entrepreneur. While retaining his sales position and the income it generated, Hal started his first business and his first additional stream of income. He provided sales coaching for both individual sales reps and sales teams. When the economy crashed in 2008, Hal's income was almost entirely dependent on his coaching business. When more than half of his clients couldn't afford to pay for his coaching, and he lost over half of his income, he swore he'd never be dependent on one source of income again.

Year by year, Hal has since added nine additional significant streams of income. These include private and group coaching programs, writing books, keynote speaking, facilitating paid masterminds, podcasting, foreign publishing, franchising and publishing books in *The Miracle Morning* book series, affiliate income, and hosting live events.

Although Hal's approach to creating multiple streams of income mentioned above is just one of countless that you could take (e.g., you could buy real estate, leverage the stock market, open brick-and-mortar stores, etc.), the important thing is that you now have the information and the knowledge to make better financial decisions during college and after graduating college. When you begin to have your first source of income, then you can make diversifying your sources of income a priority. Schedule time blocks in your schedule—one hour a day, one day a week, or a few hours every Saturday—so that you can establish additional income sources that bring you monthly income, which will provide financial security and ultimately financial freedom in the future.

Principle #4: Systematize Your World

Effective self-leaders have *systems* for just about everything from work activities (such as scheduling, exam studying, and attending meetings) to personal activities (such as sleeping, eating, managing money, and other responsibilities). Those systems make life easier and ensure you are ready for anything.

Here are a few practices you can implement immediately to begin systematizing your world:

1. Automate What You Can.

As a student, the last thing you want to do is waste time or forget to do something. That is why each night before I sleep, I clean my room, which keeps me from losing anything and creates a peaceful environment—and it takes only about 10 minutes. Then, I prepare what I am going to wear the next day, organize all of my Miracle Morning essentials, place a glass of water on my desk to help me wake up, and put all the books and notebooks I need the following day in my backpack. Creating this habit of preparing everything the night before allows me to be ready for another day of productivity!

2. Backpacks and Beyond.

Hal, in addition to being a best-selling author, is a speaker who travels week after week, sharing *The Miracle Morning* message with audiences around the country and abroad. Collecting the items he needed for every trip was time-consuming, inefficient, and ineffective because he would often forget something at home or in his office. After the third time he forgot the charger for his computer and had to find an Apple store to buy a $99 replacement (ouch) or ask the front desk for a phone charger, shaver, or an extra set of cufflinks left behind by an earlier guest, he'd had enough. He assembled a travel bag containing every item he needs for his trips, and now he can leave at a moment's notice because his bag contains everything to conduct business on the road: business cards, brochures, copies of his books, adapters, and chargers for his phone and computer. He even includes earplugs in case his hotel neighbors are noisy.

You'll know you need a system when you have a recurring challenge or find that you're missing important items because you're unprepared. If you walk out the door with just enough time to get to your first destination of the day on schedule only to discover your car is running on fumes, you need a system for getting out the door earlier. Here are some ways to plan ahead:

- Prepare your lunch, your purse or backpack, and your gym bag and lay out your clothes the night before.

- Prepare an out-of-room kit with books, notebooks, pens, calculator, computer and computer charger, or other items you need for class.

- Stash healthy snacks for when you're on the go to prevent stopping for a not-so-healthy option or being hungry.

Said another way, wherever you need to get your act together, you need a system. A life without systems is a life with unnecessary stress! This is especially true for busy college students.

3. Foundational Scheduling.

One consequence of the freedom and options for work, living, and entertainment available to us these days is that we don't necessarily know how to manage it all. Our focus, productivity, and grades may suffer from the lifestyle we desire and the tools designed to set us free and make life easy. People spend time bouncing from one task to another and then wondering what happened to the day and what, if any, significant progress was made toward what they want. Can you relate?

I am going to share something with you, or at least remind you of it, that will transform your ability to produce consistent and spectacular results in your life. You must create a foundational schedule that gives structure and intentionality to your days and weeks. A foundational schedule is a predetermined, recurring schedule that is made up of focused time blocks dedicated to your highest-priority activities.

I know, I know—imposing structure feels like the lack of freedom we work hard to avoid. Trust me, I get it. But the more you leverage a foundational schedule, consisting of time blocks dedicated to the projects or activities that will move the needle in your academic and personal life, the more freedom you'll ultimately create.

That's not to say you cannot have flexibility in your schedule. In fact, I strongly suggest that you *schedule* flexibility. Plan plenty of time blocks for friends, fun, and recreation in your calendar. You could even go so far as to include a "whatever I feel like" time block, during which you do ... whatever you feel like. You can also move the blocks as needed.

What's important is that you go through your days and weeks with a high level of clarity and intentionality with regards to how you're going to invest every hour of every day, even if that hour is spent doing whatever you feel like. At least you planned on it. Maintaining a foundational schedule is how you will maximize your productivity, so that you almost never end the day wondering where your time went. Your time won't go anywhere unless you make a conscious decision, because you'll be intentional with every minute of it.

I asked Hal to share his weekly foundational schedule with me so I could see an example of what this can look like. Although Hal has the luxury of entrepreneurial freedom and doesn't need to follow any predetermined schedule, he will tell you that having his foundational schedule in place is one of his keys to ensuring he maximizes each day. If your life has external structure, for example classes that meet at the same time each week or a job with regular hours, then you can structure your time off and probably some of your work time as well. One thing I noticed about Hal's schedule is that every hour is planned. I have made this foundational schedule based off the busy schedule I had as a full-time student living on campus studying chemistry, a Resident Advisor with a part time-job, and a member of a service organization.

COLLEGE STUDENT

TIME	MON	TUES	WED
6:00 AM	S.A.V.E.R.S.	S.A.V.E.R.S.	S.A.V.E.R.S.
7:00 AM	Academic Work Time	Academic Work Time	Academic Work Time
8:00 AM	Part-Time Job	Part-Time Job	Class
9:00 AM	↓	↓	↓
10:00 AM	Class	↓	Class
11:00 AM	↓	Lunch	↓
12:00 PM	Lunch	Class	Lunch
1:00 PM	Class	↓	Lab #1
2:00 PM	↓	Office Hours	↓
3:00 PM	↓	↓	↓
4:00 PM	Study Time (with 10 mini breaks)	Class	↓
5:00 PM	↓	↓	Early Dinner
6:00 PM	↓	Break Time	Break Time
7:00 PM	Dinner with Friends	Dinner	Quick Study Session
8:00 PM	↓	Staff Meeting	RA On Duty until 8AM
9:00 PM	↓	Study Time	RA Programming for Residence Hall
10:00 PM	Service Organization Meeting	↓	Study Time
11:00 PM	Bed	Bed	Bed

THURS	FRI	SAT/SUN
S.A.V.E.R.S.	S.A.V.E.R.S.	Sleep
Academic Work Time	Academic Work Time	**7:30 AM** S.A.V.E.R.S.
Lab #2	Class	⬇
⬇	⬇	Breakfast with Friends
⬇	Class	Volunteer
⬇	⬇	⬇
Lunch	Lunch	⬇
Part-Time Job	Break	Lunch
⬇	Finish one assignment due next week	⬇
⬇	⬇	Study Time
Study Time (with 10 mini breaks)	⬇	⬇
⬇	⬇	Early Dinner
⬇	⬇	Study Time
⬇	Go out with Friends	Family/Friends Time
RA On Duty until 8AM	⬇	⬇
Study Time	⬇	**Sat:** Out with Friends **Sun:** Plan following week
⬇	⬇	⬇
Bed	(let's be realistic here)	Sleep

Keep in mind that, as it is for everyone, things will come up that will cause the schedule to change (events, interviews, emergency meetings, more coursework, etc.), but only temporarily. As soon as those responsibilities are completed, you can fall right back into your schedule.

One of the main reasons this technique is so effective is that it takes the emotional roller coaster out of the decision making for your daily activities. How many times has an appointment or meeting gone badly and then affected your emotional state and your ability to focus for the rest of the day? Chances are it happens more often than you'd like to admit. If you followed a foundational schedule you were committed to and the calendar said "Study for exam," "Write paper," or "Fill out application for internship," then you would still have a fruitful afternoon. Take control. Stop leaving your productivity to chance and letting outside influences manage your time. Create your foundational schedule—one that incorporates everything you need to get done as well as recreational, family, and fun time—and follow through with it no matter what.

If you find you need additional support to ensure that you follow through, send a copy of your foundational schedule to an accountability partner and have them hold you accountable. Your commitment to this one system will allow you to have significantly more control over your productivity and results.

Principle #5: Commit to Consistency

If there is any not-so-obvious secret to success, this is it: *Commit to consistency.* Every result that you desire—from improving your physique to improving your grades to spending more quality time with your friends and family—requires a consistent approach to produce the desired results.

In the chapters that follow, I'll give you the insight and direction you need to take consistent action. For now, prepare your mind to keep going—even when the results you want aren't coming fast enough—and to have the stamina to withstand plenty of rejection and disappointment as you adjust to your new self. The best college students are consistent, persistent, and unfailing in their dedication to taking action every day, and you need to be the same!

HOW IS YOUR SELF-ESTEEM DOING?

As American playwright August Wilson says, "Confront the dark parts of yourself, and work to banish them with illumination and forgiveness. Your willingness to wrestle with your demons will cause your angels to sing." Self-esteem gives you the courage to try new things and the power to believe in yourself.

It is vitally important that you give yourself permission to feel proud of yourself. Yes, we need to be realistic about our weaknesses and always strive to improve, but don't hesitate to be proud of your strengths and revel in the little wins. In the meantime, many days are filled with disappointments, delays, and denials, so it is vitally important that you love yourself. If you are doing the best you can, give yourself credit. I keep a special section in my journal to write love notes to myself. On days I need a little extra encouragement, I write down all the things I love and appreciate about me.

An unstoppable self-esteem is a powerful tool. You probably already know that with a negative attitude you are going nowhere—and fast! With the right attitude, all the challenges of the day can roll off your back. You stay calm and are able to keep going. When you are confident in your abilities and committed to consistency, your behavior will change, and your success is inevitable.

PUTTING SELF-LEADERSHIP INTO ACTION

Let's review the concepts I've discussed in this chapter. I talked about the importance of self-leadership in improving your life, both personally and professionally. Developing self-leadership helps put you in the leadership role of your life as a whole. It eliminates the victim mentality and ensures you know the values, beliefs, and vision you want to live into.

Step One: Review and create a plan to integrate the Five Foundational Principles of Self-Leadership:

1. **Take 100 Percent Responsibility.** Remember, the moment you accept responsibility for everything in your life is the moment you claim the power to change anything in your life. Your success is 100 percent up to you.

2. **Prioritize Fitness and Make Exercise Enjoyable.** If daily fitness isn't already a priority in your life, make it so. In addition to your morning exercise, block time for longer, 30–60 minute workouts three to five times each week. As for which foods will give you a surplus of energy, we'll cover that in the next chapter.

3. **Aim for Financial Freedom.** Begin to take steps as a college student to develop the positive habits that will inevitably lead you to a life of financial freedom, including saving a minimum of 10 percent of your income, continuously educating yourself on the topic of money, and diversifying your sources of income.

4. **Systematize Your World.** Start by creating a foundational schedule, then identify which areas of your life or business can benefit when you put systems and time-blocked schedules in place, so that every day your result-producing processes have been predetermined and your success is virtually guaranteed. Most importantly, make sure you instill some system for accountability into your world, whether that be through a family member, roommate, or a coach, by making commitments to them and leading by example.

5. **Commit to Consistency.** Everyone needs structure. Choose consistency and commit to personal expectations and values. If you're trying a new approach, give it an extended period of time to work before throwing in the towel to try something different.

Step Two: Develop your self-control and upgrade your self-image by using affirmations and visualization. Be sure to customize both at your earliest opportunity. It takes time to see results, and the sooner you start, the sooner you'll notice improvements.

By now I hope you've gained a sense of how important your personal development is in creating success. As you continue to read this book—and I suggest you read it more than once—I recommend that you intentionally address the areas where you know you need improvement and expansion. If your self-esteem could use a boost, then take steps to elevate it. Design affirmations to increase and develop it over time. Visualize yourself acting with more confidence, raising your personal standards, and loving yourself more.

If this sounds overwhelming, remember the power of incremental change. You don't have to do everything all at once. And I've got more good news for you: In the next chapter, we're going to break down exactly how to engineer your life to create optimal levels of sustained physical, mental, and emotional energy so that you're able to maintain extraordinary levels of clarity, focus, and action, day in and day out.

— 5 —

NOT-SO-OBVIOUS COLLEGE STUDENT SUCCESS PRINCIPLE #2:

ENERGY ENGINEERING

The world belongs to the engergetic.
—RALPH WALDO EMMERSON

A s a college student, you live and die by your own steam. On some days—and I know you've had those days—you wake up, and you just don't have the energy or motivation you need to meet the challenges you know are coming. Being a college student can be exhausting, both physically and mentally—and that's on the good days. To maintain your focus on those days, in the middle of uncertainty and overwhelm, is no easy task. The good days take energy, enthusiasm, and persistence. The hard days take all that and more.

A student with low energy suffers greatly. Motivation is hard to sustain. Focus is often generated artificially by stimulants, such as a common drug of choice—caffeine. *Being a student requires an abundance of energy.* There's no way around it. You can have the best schedule, the best study partner or group, and the best action plan for the day, but if you don't have the *energy* to take advantage of them, reaching your goals is going to be unnecessarily difficult. If you want to maximize your academics, you need energy—the more the better, and the more *consistent* the better.

- Energy is the fuel that enables you to maintain clarity, focus, and action so that you can generate stellar results, day after day.

- Energy is contagious—it spreads from you to the world around you like a beneficial virus, creating symptoms of enthusiasm and positive responses everywhere.

- Energy is the foundation of everything, and it is what determines the success we attract.

The question is, *how do you strategically engineer your life to so that you maintain a high level of sustainable energy* that is always available to you, on demand?

When we struggle with energy issues, we might try to compensate with caffeine and other stimulants, and they'll work for a while … until we crash. You may have noticed the same thing. You can lean on stimulants to build up energy for a short while, but then the energy seems to fall off just when you need it the most. Can't you hear one of those infomercial hosts chime in here? *But Natalie, there's got to be a better way!*

There is …

If you've been fueling yourself on coffee and pure determination, you haven't even begun to reach the heights of achievement that are possible when you understand how energy works and commit yourself to engineering your life for optimum energy.

NATURAL ENERGY CYCLES

The first thing to understand about energy is that the goal isn't to be running at full speed all the time. That isn't practical for maintaining a constant output. As human beings, we have a natural ebb and flow to our energy levels. Being the best college student, it turns out, is the same. The trick is to marry, or at least try to sync up, your cycles with the rhythm of your workday. Know that you will need to access deeper wells of energy during particularly intense times throughout the week, month, and year, and allow yourself the time to rest, rejuvenate, and recharge when the intensity lessens.

Just like houseplants need water, our energy reserves need regular replenishing. You can go full tilt for long periods of time, but eventually your mind, body, and spirit will need to be refilled. Think of your life as a container that holds your energy. When you do not properly manage what's in your container, it's like having a hole in the bottom. No matter how much you pour in, you still won't feel fully energized.

Instead of letting yourself get to the point of being overwhelmed, burned out, or stressed out, why not become proactive about your energy levels and have an auto-recharge system in place? This will help you plug the holes in your container and allow you to fill up with the energy you need.

If you have resigned yourself to being tired, cranky, behind on your to-do list, out of shape, and unhappy, I have some great news.

Being continually exhausted is not only unacceptable, *you don't have to settle for it.* There are a few simple ways to get what you need and want—more rest, time to replenish and recharge, and inner peace and happiness. A tall order? Yes. Impossible? Heck, no!

This is about strategically engineering your life for optimum and sustainable physical, mental, and emotional energy. Here are the three principles I follow to keep my energy reserves at maximum capacity and on tap for whenever I need them.

1. Eat and Drink for Energy

When it comes to energy engineering, what you eat and drink may play the most critical role of all. If you're like most people, you base your food choices on taste first and consequences second (if you consider them at all). Yet what pleases our taste buds in the moment doesn't always give us maximum energy to last throughout the day.

There is nothing wrong with eating foods that taste good, but if you want to be truly healthy and have the energy to perform like a champion, here's the big idea: It is crucial that we make a conscious decision to **place more value on the health and energy consequences of food than we do on the taste.** Why? Because digesting food is one of the most energy-draining processes that the body endures. Need evidence? Think about how exhausted you feel after a big meal, like Thanksgiving dinner. It's no coincidence that a large meal is usually followed by heavy eyes and ultimately a nap. They call it a food coma for a reason.

Foods like bread, cooked meats, dairy products, and any foods that have been processed require more energy to digest than they contribute to your body. So, rather than giving you energy, these essentially "dead" foods tend to drain your energy to fuel digestion and leave you with an energy deficit. On the other hand, "living" foods, like raw fruits, vegetables, nuts, and seeds, typically give you more energy than they require for digestion and therefore provide your body and mind with an energy surplus, which enables you to perform at your best.

Put very simply, everything you put in your body either contributes to or detracts from your health and energy. Drinking water puts a check in the plus column; double shots of tequila won't. Eating a diet rich with fresh fruits and vegetables equals more plusses. Rolling through the drive-through to wolf down some fast food? Not so much. I know you know the drill. This isn't rocket science, but it may be the single most important area of your life to optimize. You may need to stop fooling yourself.

If you're not already doing so, it's time to be intentional and strategic about what you eat, when you eat, and—most importantly—*why* you eat so that you can engineer your life for optimum energy.

Strategic Eating

Up until this point, you may have been wondering, *When do I get to eat during my Miracle Morning?!* I'll cover that here. I'll also share what to eat for maximum energy, which is critical, and why the *reason* you choose to eat what you eat may be the most important consideration of all.

When to Eat—Again, remember that digesting food uses a lot of energy each day. The bigger the meal, the more food you give your body to digest, the more drained you will feel. With that in mind, I recommend eating your first meal after your Miracle Morning. This ensures that, for optimum alertness and focus during the S.A.V.E.R.S., your blood will be flowing to your brain rather than to your stomach to digest your food.

However, I do recommend starting your day by ingesting a small amount of healthy fats as fuel for your brain. Studies show that keeping your mind sharp and your moods in balance may be largely related to the type of fat you eat. "Our brain is at least 60 percent fat, and it's composed of fats (like omega-3s) that must be obtained from the diet," says Amy Jamieson-Petonic, M.Ed., a registered dietitian, the director of wellness coaching at the Cleveland Clinic, and a national spokesperson for the American Dietetic Association.

After drinking his first full glass of water, Hal starts every morning with a tablespoon of organic coconut butter (specifically *Nutiva Organic Coconut Manna*, which you can order from Amazon.com) and a large mug of organic coffee, which he blends with Bulletproof Cacao Butter (available on Bulletproof.com). The tablespoon of coconut butter is such a small amount that it's easily digested, and it contains enough healthy fats to provide fuel for the brain. The health benefits of cacao are significant, from lowering blood pressure to being a powerhouse full of antioxidants (cacao rates in the top 20 on the oxygen radical absorbance capacity, or ORAC, scale, which is used to rate the antioxidant capacity of foods).

Maybe the most exciting fact is that eating cacao actually makes you happy! It contains phenylethylamine (known as the "love drug"), which is responsible for the state of our mood and the same feelings you get when you are in love. It also acts as a stimulant and can improve mental alertness. In other words, cacao equals win, win, win!

If you feel that you must eat a meal first thing in the morning, make sure that it's a small, light, and easily digestible meal, such as fresh fruit or a smoothie (more on that in a minute).

Why to Eat—Let's take a moment to delve deeper into why you choose to eat the foods that you do. When you're shopping at the grocery store or selecting food from a menu at a restaurant, what criteria do you use to determine which foods you are going to put in your body? Are your choices based purely on taste? Texture? Convenience? Are they based on health? Energy? Dietary restrictions?

Most people choose the foods they eat based solely on the taste, and at a deeper level because of an emotional attachment to the foods they like the taste of. If you were to ask someone why they eat ice cream or fried chicken, or drink soda, they would most likely say that they love ice cream, were in the mood for fried chicken, or like drinking soda. All of these answers are based on the emotional enjoyment derived primarily from the way these foods taste. In this case, a person is not likely to explain their food choices with how much value these foods will add to their health, or how much sustained energy they'll receive as a result of ingesting them.

My point is this: if we want to have more energy (which we all do), and if we want our lives to be healthy and disease-free (which we all do), then it is crucial that we reexamine why we eat the foods that we do. From this point forward—and I know I've covered this, but it bears repeating—start placing significantly more value on the health and energy consequences of the foods you eat than you do on the taste. The taste provides you with only a few minutes of pleasure, but the health and energy consequences impact the rest of your day and the rest of your life.

In no way am I saying that we should eat foods that don't taste good in exchange for the health and energy benefits. I'm saying that we can have both. If we want to live every day with an abundance of energy so we can perform at our best and live long, healthy lives, we must choose to eat more foods that are good for our health and give us sustained energy as well as taste great.

What to Eat—Before we talk about what to eat, let's take a second to talk about what to drink. Remember that Step #4 of the 5-Step Snooze-Proof Wake-Up Strategy is to drink a full glass of water first thing in the morning so you can rehydrate and reenergize after a full night of sleep.

Next, like Hal, I typically brew a cup of Bulletproof Coffee before I start my Miracle Morning. I set my alarm 15 minutes early to give myself time to make my coffee without intruding on my time for the S.A.V.E.R.S.

As for what to eat, it has been proven that a diet rich in living foods such as fresh fruits and vegetables will greatly increase your energy levels, improve your mental focus and emotional wellbeing, keep you healthy, and protect you from disease. Hal created the Miracle Morning "Super-Food Smoothie" that incorporates everything your body needs in one tall, frosty glass! I'm talking about complete protein (all the essential amino acids), age-defying antioxidants, Omega 3 essential fatty acids (to boost immunity, cardiovascular health, and brain power), plus a rich spectrum of vitamins and minerals ... and that's just for starters. I haven't even mentioned all the superfoods, such as the stimulating, mood-lifting phytonutrients in cacao (the tropical bean from which chocolate is made), the long-lasting energy of Maca (the Andean adaptogen revered for its hormone-balancing effects), and the immune-boosting nutrients and appetite-suppressing properties of chia seeds.

The Miracle Morning Super-Food Smoothie not only provides you with sustained energy, it also tastes great. You might even find that it enhances your ability to create miracles in your everyday life. You can download and print the recipe for free at www.TMMBook.com.

Remember the old saying "you are what you eat"? Food provides the building blocks and the fuel your body needs to do all the amazing things it does. Take care of your body so your body will take care of you. You will feel vibrant energy and enhanced clarity immediately!

Let's talk about fuel. I have shifted my view of food from that of a reward, treat, or comfort to that of fuel. I want to eat delicious, healthy foods that boost my energy levels and allow me to keep going as long as I need and want to go.

Don't get me wrong. I still enjoy certain foods that are not the healthiest choices, but I strategically reserve them for times when I don't need to maintain optimal energy levels, such as in the evenings and on weekends.

The easiest way to start making better decisions about eating is to start paying attention to the way you feel after eating certain foods. I started setting a timer for 60 minutes after I finished each meal. When my timer went off, I assessed my energy level. It didn't take long for me to recognize which foods gave me the biggest power boost and which ones didn't. I can clearly tell the difference in my energy level on the days when I drink a smoothie or eat a salad and the days I cave for a chicken sandwich or some of that pizza that smells so good. The former give me a surplus of energy; the latter put me in an energy deficit.

What would it be like to give your body what it needs to work and play for as long as you like? What would it be like to give yourself exactly what you truly deserve? Give yourself the gift of great health, consciously chosen through what you eat and drink.

If you are eating throughout the day almost as an afterthought, maybe hitting a drive-through after you've passed the point of being famished, it is time to start building a new strategy.

Ask yourself the following questions:

- Can I start to consciously consider the consequences of what I eat (both health and energy consequences) and value that above the taste?

- Can I keep water with me at all times so that I can hydrate with intention and purpose and avoid becoming dehydrated?

- Can I plan my meals in advance, including incorporating healthy snacks, so I can combat any patterns I have that don't serve me?

Yes, you can do all of these and much more. Think about how much better your life will be and how much more energy you will have for your work when you become conscious and intentional about your eating and drinking habits.

- You will easily maintain a positive mental and emotional state. Low energy causes us to feel down, whereas high energy levels produce a positive state of mind, outlook, and attitude.

- You will be more disciplined. Low energy drains our willpower, making us more likely to choose the easy things over the right things. High energy levels increase self-discipline.

- You will set an example for the people you lead and the people you love. How we live our lives gives permission to those around us to do the same.

- You will get healthier, feel much better, and live longer.

- Bonus—You will settle at your natural weight effortlessly.

- Best Bonus Ever—You'll do better in your academics and all your extracurricular activities because you'll look and feel great!

Don't forget to stay hydrated throughout the day. Lack of water can lead to dehydration, a condition that occurs when you don't have enough water in your body to carry out normal functions. Even mild dehydration can drain your energy and make you tired.

By implementing the Five-Step Snooze-Proof Wake-Up Strategy, you'll have had your first glass of water at the start of the day. Beyond that, I recommend keeping a large water bottle with you at all times and make a habit of drinking 16 ounces every one to two hours. If remembering to drink is a challenge for you, set a recurring timer to trigger the habit to finish your water bottle and refill it for the next round of rehydration.

When it comes to frequency of eating, it's important to refuel every three to four hours with small, easily digestible, living foods. I intentionally refuel every three to four hours during the day. My regular meals consist of some form of protein and vegetables. To keep my blood glucose levels from dropping, I snack frequently on living foods, including raw fruits and nuts, and one of my favorite go-to snacks—kale chips. I try to plan my best meals for the days I need to be the most productive.

I believe that eating for energy—from my first meal of the day until I'm done working—combined with exercise also gives me the freedom to eat what I want in the evenings and on weekends. I believe I can eat whatever I want, just not always as much as I'd like. I've learned to taste everything but eat just enough that I'm satisfied.

In the end, here is the simple thing to remember: Food is fuel. We should use it to get us from the beginning of the day all the way to the end, feeling great and having plenty of energy. Placing more value on the energy consequences of the foods you eat, above the taste, and eating foods that fuel energy are the first steps in energy engineering.

2. Sleep and Wake to Win

Sleep more to achieve more. That might be the most counterintuitive mantra you'll ever hear, but it's true. The body needs enough shut-eye each night to function properly and to recharge after a demanding day. Sleep also plays a critical role in immune function, metabolism, memory, learning, and other vital bodily functions. It's when the body does the majority of its repairing, healing, resting, and growing.

If you don't sleep enough, you're gradually wearing yourself down and limiting your ability to grow in any part of your life.

Sleeping Versus Sleeping Enough

But how much is enough? There is a big difference between the amount of sleep you can get by on and the amount you need to function optimally. Researchers at the University of California, San Francisco discovered that some people have a gene that enables them to do well on six hours of sleep a night. This gene, however, is very rare, appearing in less than 3 percent of the population. For the other 97 percent of us, six hours doesn't come close to cutting it. Just because you're able to function on five to six hours of sleep doesn't mean you wouldn't feel a lot better and actually get more done if you spent an extra hour or two in bed.

As I said, that may sound counterintuitive. You might be thinking, *Spend more time in bed and get more done? How does that work?* But it has been well documented that enough sleep allows the body to function at higher levels of performance. You'll not only work better and faster, but your attitude will improve, too.

The amount of rest each individual needs every night differs, but research shows that the average adult needs approximately seven to eight hours of sleep to restore the energy it takes to handle all the demands of living each day.

I have been conditioned, as many of us have, to think I need eight to ten hours of sleep. In fact, sometimes I need less, and sometimes I need more. The best way to figure out if you're meeting your sleep needs is to evaluate how you feel as you go about your day. If you're logging enough hours, you'll feel energetic and alert all day long, from the moment you wake up until your regular bedtime. If you're not, you'll reach for caffeine or sugar midmorning or midafternoon … or both.

If you're like most people, when you don't get enough rest, you have difficulty concentrating, thinking clearly, and even remembering things. You might notice your ineffectiveness or inefficiencies at home or at school, or even blame these missteps on your busy schedule. The more sleep you miss, the more pronounced your symptoms become.

In addition, a lack of rest and relaxation can really work a number on your mood. School is no place for crankiness! It is a scientific fact that when individuals miss out on good nightly rest, their personalities are affected, and they are generally grumpier, less patient, and more likely to snap at people. The result of missing out on critical, much-needed rest might make you a bear to be around, which is not much fun for anyone, yourself included.

Most adults cut back on their sleep to pack more activities into their day. As you run against the clock to beat deadlines, you might be tempted to skimp on sleep to get more done. Unfortunately, lack of sleep can cause the body to run down, which allows illness, viruses, and diseases the tiny opening they need to attack the body. When you are sleep-deprived, your immune system can become compromised, and is susceptible to just about anything. Eventually, lack of rest can cause illness that leads to missed days or even weeks of class. That's no way to attempt improving your academic performance.

On the flip side, when you get enough sleep, your body runs as it should, you're pleasant to be around, and your immune system is stronger. And that's precisely when you'll get better grades and attract more success into your professional life. Think of good sleep as the time when you turn on your inner magnet. Wake up rested and in a great mood because of your S.A.V.E.R.S., and you'll do well in your classes—because a well-rested student is also a successful one.

The True Benefits of Sleep

You may not realize how powerful sleep actually is. While you're happily wandering through your dreams, sleep is doing some hard work on your behalf and delivering a host of amazing benefits.

Improve your memory. Your mind is surprisingly busy while you snooze. During sleep you clean out damaging toxins that are byproducts of brain function during the day, strengthen memories, and practice skills learned while you were awake through a process called consolidation.

"If you are trying to learn something, whether it's physical or mental, you learn it to a certain point with practice," says Dr. David

Rapoport, who is an associate professor at NYU Langone Medical Center and a sleep expert, "but something happens while you sleep that makes you learn it better."

In other words, if you're trying to learn something new, whether it's Spanish, a new tennis swing, or the concepts of an exam coming up, you'll perform better when you get adequate sleep.

Live longer. Too much or too little sleep is associated with a shorter life span, although it's not clear if it's a cause or an effect. In a 2010 study of women ages 50–79, more deaths occurred in women who got fewer than five hours or more than six-and-a-half hours of sleep per night. Getting the right amount of sleep is a good idea for your long-term health.

Be more creative. While sleep improves memory and learning, REM sleep in particular seems to boost your ability to solve problems creatively. Researchers from Harvard studied sleepers before and after naps. As a control, they put other participants through the same battery of questions without a nap. Some of the sleeping participants were allowed to slip into REM sleep while others were denied the pleasure. Nappers who slept more deeply enhanced their creative problem-solving performance by nearly 40 percent when compared to their counterparts who slept for less time and those who didn't sleep at all.

Attain and maintain a healthy weight more easily. If you're overweight, you won't have the same energy levels as those at a healthy weight. Along with changing your lifestyle to include more exercise and better diet with your Miracle Morning practice and Energy Engineering, you'll want to plan an earlier bedtime. Putting additional physical demands on your body means you will need to counterbalance those demands with plenty of rest.

Researchers with the University of Chicago found that dieters who were well-rested lost more fat—up to 56 percent more—than those who were sleep-deprived, who lost more muscle mass. Participants' hunger actually increased when they lacked sufficient shut-eye. The key connection between sleep and metabolism is their brain connection: The same sectors of the brain control both functions.

Hormones that happen to increase your appetite are released when you don't get enough sleep.

Feel less stressed. This probably isn't news to you: A good night's rest reduces your stress. Diminished sleep and stress affect cardiovascular health to further impact your long-term health and short-term energy supply. Along with cutting your stress, your commitment to sleep allows the body to better control blood pressure. It is also believed that sleep affects cholesterol levels, which play a significant role in heart disease.

Avoid mistakes and accidents. The National Highway Traffic Safety Administration reports that fatigue is responsible for most "fatal, single-car, run-off-the-road crashes due to the driver's performance." What's more shocking is that driver fatigue is cited in these crashes more often than alcohol! This is because lack of sleep affects reaction time and decision-making, which is a dangerous combination on the road.

If insufficient sleep for only one night can be as detrimental to your driving ability as having an alcoholic drink, imagine how it affects your ability to maintain the focus necessary to become a top student.

So, how many hours of sleep do you *really* need? Only you truly know how much sleep you need in order to hit home run after home run. If you struggle with falling or staying asleep, and it is a concern for you, I highly recommend reading Shawn Stevenson's book, *Sleep Smarter: 21 Proven Tips to Sleep Your Way to a Better Body, Better Health, and Bigger Success.* It's one of the best-written and most-researched books that I've seen on the topic of sleep.

Getting consistent and effective rest is as critical to performing at your best as what you eat. A good night's sleep provides the basis for a day of clear thought, sustained energy, peak performance, and maximum creativity for the problems that arise during the day. Commit to getting enough sleep with a consistent bedtime, because what may be even more important than how many hours of sleep you get each night is how you approach the act of waking up in the morning.

How Much Sleep Do We Really Need?

The first thing some experts will tell you about how many hours of sleep we need is that there is no universal number. The ideal length of nighttime sleep varies among people, and is influenced by factors such as age, genetics, stress, overall health, how much exercise a person gets, diet—including how late we consumed our last meal—and countless other factors.

For example, if your diet consists of fast food, processed foods, excessive sugar, etc., then your body will be challenged to recharge and rejuvenate while you sleep. It will work long into the night to detoxify and filter out the poisons that you've put into it. When you eat a clean diet of living food, as we covered in the last section, then your body will rest more easily. The person who eats a clean diet will almost always wake feeling refreshed and with more energy, able to function optimally even with less sleep, than the person who eats poorly.

Since there is such a wide variety of opposing evidence from countless studies and experts, and since the amount of sleep needed varies from person to person, I'm not going to attempt to make a case that there is one right approach to sleep. Instead, I'll share my own real-world results from personal experience and experimentation, and from studying the sleep habits of some of the greatest minds in history. I'll warn you that some of this may be somewhat controversial.

How to Wake Up With More Energy (On Less Sleep)

Through experimenting with various sleep durations—as well as learning those of many other Miracle Morning practitioners who have tested this theory—Hal found that how our sleep affects our biology is largely affected by our own personal belief about how much sleep we need. In other words, how we feel when we wake up in the morning— and this is a very important distinction—is not based solely on how many hours of sleep we got, but significantly influenced by what we told ourselves we were going to feel when we woke up.

For example, if you believe that you need eight hours of sleep to feel rested, but you're getting into bed at midnight and have to wake up at 6:00 a.m., you're likely to tell yourself, "I'm going to feel exhausted in the morning." What happens as soon as your alarm clock goes off, you open your eyes, and you realize it's time to wake up? What's the first thought that you think? It's the same thought you had before bed! "Geez, I only got six hours of sleep. I feel exhausted." It's a self-fulfilling, self-sabotaging prophecy. If you tell yourself you're going to feel tired in the morning, then you are absolutely going to feel tired. If you believe that you need eight hours to feel fully rested, then you're not going to feel rested on anything less. But what if you changed your beliefs?

The mind-body connection is a powerful thing, and I believe we must take responsibility for every aspect of our lives, including the power to wake up every day feeling energized, regardless of how many hours of sleep we get.

You Snooze, You Lose: The Truth About Waking Up

The old saying, "you snooze, you lose" has a much deeper meaning than any of us realized. When you hit the snooze button and delay waking up until you must—meaning you wait until the time when you have to be somewhere, do something, or take care of someone else—consider that you're starting your day with resistance. Every time you hit the snooze button, you're in a state of resistance to your day, to your life, and to waking up and creating the life you say you want.

According to Robert S. Rosenberg, medical director of the Sleep Disorders Centers of Prescott Valley and Flagstaff, Arizona, "When you hit the snooze button repeatedly, you're doing two negative things to yourself. First, you're fragmenting what little extra sleep you're getting so it is of poor quality. Second, you're starting to put yourself through a new sleep cycle that you aren't giving yourself enough time to finish. This can result in persistent grogginess throughout the day."

If you're not already, make sure you start following the Five-Minute Snooze-Proof Wake-Up Strategy in chapter 2, and you'll be poised to win. If getting to bed on time is your challenge, try setting a "bedtime alarm" that sounds an hour before your ideal bedtime, prompting you to start winding down so you can hit the sack. This will give you an advantage when it comes time to rise and shine, the time when you can set yourself up to make the most of your day.

When you wake up each day with passion and purpose, you join the small percentage of high achievers who are living their dreams. Most importantly, you will be happy. By simply changing your approach to waking up in the morning, you will change everything. But don't take my word for it—trust these famous early risers: Oprah Winfrey, Tony Robbins, Bill Gates, Howard Schultz, Deepak Chopra, Wayne Dyer, Thomas Jefferson, Benjamin Franklin, Albert Einstein, Aristotle, and far too many more to list here.

No one ever taught us that by learning how to consciously set our intention to wake up each morning with a genuine desire—even enthusiasm—to do so, we can change our entire lives.

If you're snoozing each morning until the last possible moment when you have to head into the work of your day and then coming home and zoning out in front of the television until you go to bed (this used to be my daily routine), I've got to ask you this: *When are you going to develop yourself into the person you need to be to create the levels of health, wealth, happiness, success, and freedom that you truly want and deserve? When are you going to live your life instead of numbly going through the motions looking for every possible distraction to escape reality? What if your reality—your life—could finally be something that you can't wait to be conscious for? And what if that all starts with how you wake up?*

There is no better day than today for you to give up who we've been for who you can become, and upgrade the life you've been living for the one you really want. There is no better book than the one you are holding in your hands to show you how to become the person you need to be—one who is capable of quickly attracting, creating, and sustaining the life you have always wanted.

3. Rest to Recharge

The conscious counterpart to sleep is *rest*. While some people use the terms interchangeably, they're really quite different. You might get eight hours of sleep, but if you spend all of your waking hours on the go, then you won't have time to think or recharge your physical, mental, and emotional batteries. When you work all day, run from activity to activity after hours, and then finish with a quick dinner and late bedtime, you don't allow for a period of rest.

Likewise, spending weekends doing homework, volunteering, heading out to see a football game, going to church, singing in the choir, attending parties, etc., can do more harm than good. While each of these activities is great, maintaining a fully-packed schedule doesn't allow for time to recharge.

We live in a culture that perpetuates the belief that when our days are busy and exciting, we are more valuable, more important, or more alive. In truth, we are all of those things when we can be at peace within our own skin. Despite our best intentions to live balanced lives, the modern world demands that we are almost always connected and productive, and these demands can drain us emotionally, spiritually, and physically.

What if, instead of being constantly on the go, you valued intentional quiet time, sacred space, and periods of purposeful silence? How might that improve your life, your physical and emotional well-being, and your ability to achieve academically?

It may seem counterintuitive to take time out when your to-do list is a mile long, but the fact is that more rest is a prerequisite for truly productive work.

Research proves that rest melts your stress away. Practices like yoga and meditation also lower your heart rate, blood pressure, and oxygen consumption. They alleviate hypertension, arthritis, insomnia, depression, infertility, cancer, and anxiety. The spiritual benefits of resting are profound. Slowing down and getting quiet means you can actually hear the wisdom and knowledge of your own inner voice. Rest and its close sibling, relaxation, allow us to reconnect with the world in and around us, inviting ease and a sense of contentment into our lives.

And yes, in case you're wondering, you'll be more productive, nicer to your friends and family members (not to mention your professors and coworkers), and in general much happier as well. When we rest, it's like letting the earth lie fallow rather than constantly planting and harvesting. Our personal batteries need to be recharged. The best way to recharge them is to truly and simply rest.

Easy Ways to Rest

Most of us confuse rest with recreation. To rest, we do things like hike, garden, work out, or even party. Any of these activities can only be termed restful because it is a break from work, but truthfully it is not, and cannot, be defined as rest.

Rest has been defined as a kind of waking sleep experienced while you are alert and aware. Rest is the essential bridge to sleep, and we achieve rest and sleep the same way: by making space for and allowing it to happen. Every living organism needs rest, including you. When we don't take the time to rest, eventually its absence takes a toll on the body.

- If you are now investing five or more minutes each morning during your S.A.V.E.R.S. to meditate or sit in silence, that is a great start.

- You can reserve one night of the week for rest. You can read, watch a movie, do something low-key with friends or family, or even spend time alone.

- When you're driving, drive in silence: turn off the radio and stow your phone.

- Go for a walk without your earbuds in. Time in nature without intention or goals such as burning calories can feel like rest.

- Turn off the television. Designate a half-hour, an hour, or even half a day for silence.

- Try taking regular conscious breaths during which you focus on the inhale and exhale or the space between breaths.

- You can also mindfully drink a cup of tea, read something inspirational, write in your journal, take a hot bath, or get a massage.

- Attend a retreat. It could be with your classmates, co-workers, a group of friends, your church, any community with which you are involved, family, your spouse, or on your own in nature.

Even taking a nap is a powerful way to rest and recharge. If I'm feeling drained during the day for some reason and still have a long day ahead, I won't hesitate to hit the reset button with a 20- or 30-minute power nap. Napping can also lead to better sleep patterns.

It's helpful to set a specific time for rest. Put boundaries around it so you can claim that time.

The Rest Habit

As a student, you're in the trenches by default. You'll need to schedule your time for rest and self-care in the same way you schedule the other commitments in your life. The energy you get back will reward you many times over.

Rest certainly isn't something we were taught in school, and it may not come naturally at first. After all, you're a college student. So, you may find that you need to consciously make it a priority. Learning different mindfulness practices and bringing them into your everyday life is an effective way to deeply rest your body, mind, and spirit. Practices such as midday meditation, yoga, and purposeful silence are powerful ways to go within and achieve restful states of being, particularly when you commit to doing them regularly.

The more you integrate periods of rest and silence into your daily life, the bigger the payoff will be. During more tranquil periods, perhaps you won't need to rest as much, but periods of intensity (such as meeting a huge quota or a big deadline) may require more rest and silence than usual.

Combining exercise, healthy food choices, consistent sleep, and rest will give you a quantum leap in the right direction for you and your academics. Keep in mind that when you try to adopt these three practices—to eat, sleep, and rest more effectively—you may at first find the process uncomfortable. You may encounter some resistance. Counteract the urge to run from the discomfort by making a commitment to begin putting them into practice today.

PUTTING ENERGY ENGINEERING INTO ACTION

Step One: Commit to eating and drinking for energy by prioritizing the energy consequences of the foods you eat above the taste. After your initial glass of water in the morning, ingest some form of healthy fat to fuel your brain. Try incorporating one new healthy meal of living foods in your diet each day. Instead of snacking on potato chips, try kale chips or fresh organic fruit. And remember to keep water with you at all times so that you stay hydrated.

Step Two: Sleep and wake to win by choosing a consistent daily bedtime *and* wake-up time. Based on the time you rise for your Miracle Morning, back your way into a bedtime that ensures that you will get enough sleep. Maintain a specific bedtime for a few weeks to get your body acclimated. If you need a little nudge to get to bed on time, set an alarm that prompts you to start winding down one hour before bedtime. After a couple of weeks, feel free to play with the number of hours you leave for sleeping to optimize your energy levels.

Step Three: In addition to your Miracle Morning routine, incorporate time into your daily calendar to rest and recharge, whether that's meditation, a nap, going for a walk, or doing an activity that brings you joy. Hal takes a two-hour lunch break every day, which gives him time to play basketball or wakeboard—two activities that he loves to do and that thoroughly reenergize him. What activities can you plan for your day that will reenergize you?

—6—

NOT-SO-OBVIOUS COLLEGE STUDENT SUCCESS PRINCIPLE #3:

UNWAVERING FOCUS

The successful warrior is the average man, with laser-like focus.
—BRUCE LEE

We've all met that person. You know—*that* person. The one who runs marathons, volunteers at the local middle school, has an awesome internship, and maybe writes a novel on the side. And on top of all that? She's an incredible student, winning awards and knocking it out of the park when it comes to school, year after year. I bet you know someone like that—someone who seems unexplainably productive.

Or maybe you know *this* person—the student who runs a million clubs on campus, but never seems to be working at it. He's always playing basketball or out with his friends in the middle of the workweek. He's fit, happy, and makes every person he comes in contact with feel like a million bucks.

What you might not realize, though, is exactly how people like this do it. Maybe you thought they were lucky. Or gifted. Or connected. Or had the right personality. Or were born with superpowers!

While those things can help when it comes to being a college student, I know from experience that the real superpower behind every unbelievably productive person is *Unwavering Focus*. Unwavering Focus is the ability to maintain clarity about your highest priorities, take all the energy you've learned to generate for yourself, channel it into what matters most, and keep it there, regardless of what is going on around you or how you feel. This ability is key to becoming an exceptional college student.

When you harness the power of focus, you don't become superhuman, but you can achieve seemingly superhuman results. And the reasons for this are surprisingly straightforward.

- **Unwavering Focus makes you more effective.** Being effective doesn't mean doing the most things or doing things the fastest. It means doing the right things. You engage in the activities that create forward momentum toward your life's goals.

- **Unwavering Focus makes you more efficient.** Being efficient means doing things with the fewest resources, such as time, energy, or money. Every time your mind wanders away from your goals, you waste those things—particularly time. In school, time is always in demand, so every moment that your focus wavers is another moment lost.

- **Unwavering Focus makes you productive.** Understand that just because you're *busy* does not mean you're productive. In fact, struggling college students are usually the busiest. Too often we confuse being busy with being productive. With the former, you engage in activities that don't produce results, like checking email excessively, cleaning your car, or reorganizing your to-do list for the twelfth time this month. When you have a clear vision, identify your highest priorities, and consistently execute your most leveraged activities, you'll go from being busy to being productive.

By taking the steps that we're about to cover, you'll learn how to develop the habit of unwavering focus and join the ranks of the most productive college students in the world.

If you combine those benefits, you will achieve *a lot* more. Perhaps the greatest value of focus is that rather than scattering your energy across multiple areas of your life and getting mediocre results across the board, you will release untapped potential *and* improve your life.

Now let's turn your Miracle Morning to the task. Here are four steps you need to add to your life, in addition to your Miracle Morning, for sustained focus.

1. Find Your Best Environment(s) for Unwavering Focus.

Let's start here: *You need an environment that supports your commitment to unwavering focus.* It might be your spare bedroom, or it could be your backyard. No matter how modest, though, you need a place where you go to focus.

Part of the reason for this is simple logistics. If your materials are scattered from the trunk of your car to the kitchen counter, you can't be effective. A bigger reason, however, is that **having a place where you focus triggers the habit of focusing**. Sit at the same desk to do great work at the same time every day, and soon enough you'll find yourself slipping into the zone just by sitting down in that chair.

If you're on the road a lot, then your car, your backpack, your room, the library, and possibly campus coffee shops are part of your focus space, too. Build habits for how you pack and work on the road, and you can trigger great focus the same way you do at the office. When you are prepared and always have with you exactly what you need, you can work anywhere.

2. Clear the Unfocused Clutter.

Clutter is a focus killer, and it's our next stop on the journey. There is a reason that Marie Kondo's book, *The Life-Changing Magic of Tidying Up*, is one of the best-selling nonfiction books of the last decade. You will inspire a calm, motivated mindset when you declutter both your physical and mental space.

There are two kinds of clutter, mental and physical, and we all have them both. We carry around thoughts like these: *My sister's birthday is coming up. I have to get her a gift and card. I had a great time at dinner the other night. I need to send the host a thank-you note. I have to answer the email from my professor before I leave my room today.*

Then there are the physical items we accumulate: stacks of paper, old magazines, sticky notes, clothes we never wear, the pile of junk in the room. The trinkets, knickknacks, and tokens that accumulate as we go through life.

Clutter of either type creates the equivalent of a heavy fog, but to become focused, you need to be able to *see*. To clear your vision, you'll want to get those mental items out of your head and collected so you can relieve the mental stress of trying to remember them. And then you'll want to get those physical items out of your way, too.

Here's a simple process to help you clear the fog and create the clarity you need to focus.

- **Create a master to-do list.** You probably have lots of things that haven't been written down yet—start with those. And all those sticky notes that clutter your desk, computer screen, planner, countertops, refrigerator … Are there other places? Put those notes and action items on your master list. Put them all in one central location, whether that's a physical journal or a list on your phone, so that you can clear your mental storage. Feeling better? Keep going! We're just getting started.

- **Purge your workspace.** Schedule a half (or full) day to go through every stack of paper, file folder stuffed with documents, and tray full of unopened mail in your office. You get the gist. Throw out or shred what you don't need. Scan or file the ones that matter. Make note of any items that need your attention and cannot be delegated in your journal, then pick a time in your schedule to complete them.

- **Declutter your life.** Wherever possible, clean up and clear out every drawer, closet, cabinet, and trunk that doesn't give you a sense of calm and peace when you see it. This includes your car. This might take a few hours or a few days. Schedule a short time each day until everything is complete. Saying "I just need a weekend to declutter" is a sure way to never start. Pick a single drawer and start there. You'll be surprised at how the small bursts of work will make a big difference in your environment. Try S. J. Scott and Barrie Davenport's book, *10-Minute Declutter: The Stress-Free Habit for Simplifying Your Home,* for suggestions.

Getting physically and mentally organized will allow you to focus at a level you would never have believed possible. It will leave your energy with nowhere to go except into what *matters*.

3. Protect Yourself from Interruptions.

In addition to Hal's coaching and speaking business, he leads the COO Alliance, is an author with several works in progress, and is married with two children. As you can imagine, his time is critically important to him, just as I'm sure yours is to you.

If he were to allow constant interruptions, it would be impossible to direct his attention to what's most important at any given moment. To avoid distraction and ensure he remains focused, he keeps his phone set on Do Not Disturb. This blocks all incoming calls, texts, or notifications for email and social media. This is a simple thing that dramatically increases his daily productivity and ability to remain focused on the task at hand. I recommend returning phone calls and emails at predesignated times, according to your own schedule, not everybody else's.

You can apply the same philosophy and strategies to any notifications or alerts, as well as to your availability for colleagues, bosses, and even your professors. *Do Not Disturb* isn't just a setting on your phone. Let your friends know when you're available and when they need to leave you undisturbed.

4. Build a Foundation for Unwavering Focus.

Once you identify your focus place and begin the process of decluttering your life and guarding against interruptions, you should experience a remarkable increase in focus.

Now, it's time to take things to the next level. I use three questions to improve my focus.

1. What's working that I should *keep doing* (or do more of)?
2. What do I need to *start doing* to accelerate results?
3. What do I need to *stop doing* immediately that's holding me back from going to the next level?

If you can answer those three questions and take action on the results, you'll discover a whole new level of productivity you probably didn't think was possible. Let's look at each question in detail.

WHAT DO YOU NEED TO KEEP DOING (OR DO MORE OF)?

Let's face it, not all college student tactics and strategies are created equal. Some work better than others. Some work for a while and then become less effective. Some even make things worse.

Right now, you're probably doing a lot of the right activities, and you'll be nodding right along as you read the coming chapters on Level 10 College Student Success. If you already know the things you're doing that are working, jot those down. Perhaps you're already eating energy-rich foods, for example. Put that on the "what's working" list.

Make sure you're choosing things that actually contribute to increasing your success as a college student. It's easy to keep the things you *like* doing, but you need to make sure that the activities you're doing are directly related to becoming more successful as a student. Consider the 80/20 Rule (originally the Pareto principle), which shows that roughly 80 percent of our results come from 20 percent of our efforts. Which 20 percent of your activities impact 80 percent of your results?

Capture the activities that are working in your journal. (Among them, I hope, will be that you've started doing the Life S.A.V.E.R.S.) Everything that's on that list is a *keep doing* until it's replaced by something even more effective.

For all of the activities on your list you want to keep doing, make sure you're completely honest with yourself about *what you need to be doing more of* (in other words, what you're currently not doing enough of). If it's something you think you should be doing but it's not moving you forward toward your important goals, it doesn't belong on your list. Perfection is not one of the goals here. Overworking yourself is ultimately unproductive and takes your focus off the important things.

Keep doing what's working, and, depending on how much more you want to achieve, simply do *more* of what's working.

WHAT DO YOU NEED TO START DOING?

Once you've captured what's working and determined what you need to do more of, it's time to decide what else you can do to accelerate your success.

I have a few exceptional suggestions to prime the pump and get you started.

- Conduct weekly roommate meetings
- Eat nutrient-dense foods
- Go to professors' office hours
- Tell friends when you are available and unavailable
- Organize everything you need the night before for the next day

- Say "No" to extra-curricular activities that are not helping you reach your goals

- Create your *Foundational Schedule*—a recurring, ideally weekly schedule with a time-blocked calendar—so that every day when you wake up your highest priorities are already predetermined and planned. Then, make any necessary adjustments on Sunday night for the following week.

- Search for internships that will help you learn and grow

- Have whatever materials you might need on hand at all times

- Write down daily gratitudes

I caution you not to become overwhelmed here. Keep in mind that Rome wasn't built in a day. You don't need to identify 58 action items and implement them by tomorrow. The great thing about having a daily scribing practice as part of your Miracle Morning is that you can capture every action item over time. **Then, one or two at a time, add them to your success toolbox until they become habits.** Incremental improvements have a magical way of accumulating.

WHAT DO YOU NEED TO STOP DOING?

By now you've most likely added a few items to start doing. If you're wondering where the time is going to come from, this might be your favorite step of all. It's time to let go of the things you've been doing that don't serve you to make room for the ones that do.

I'm fairly sure you do a number of daily activities you will be relieved to stop doing, thankful to delegate to someone else, or grateful to release.

Why not stop ...

- eating unhealthy, energy-draining foods that suck the life and motivation out of you?

- doing unnecessary household chores?

- replying to texts and emails instantly?

- answering the phone? (Let it go to voicemail and reply when the timing works best for you.)
- reading and posting on social media?
- watching hours of television or Netflix a day?
- beating yourself up or worrying about what you can't change?
- committing to an extracurricular activity that is not serving your goals, health, and happiness?

Or, if you want to improve your focus dramatically in one simple step, try this easy fix: *Stop responding to buzzes and sounds like a trained seal.*

Do you really need to be alerted when you receive texts, emails, and social media notifications? Nope, didn't think so. Go into the settings of your phone, tablet, and computer, and turn all your notifications OFF.

Technology exists for your benefit, and you can take control of it this very minute. How often you check your phone messages, texts, and email can and should be decided by *you.* Let's face it, most of us do not have jobs that will result in a life-or-death situation if we do not respond immediately to a call, text, or email. We don't need to be accessible 24/7/365 except to our significant others and children. An effective alternative is to schedule times during the day to check on what's happening, what needs your immediate attention, what items can be added to your schedule or master to-do list, and what can be deleted, ignored, or forgotten.

FINAL THOUGHTS ON UNWAVERING FOCUS

Focus is like a muscle that you build over time. As with building a muscle, you need to show up and do the work to make it grow. Cut yourself some slack if you falter, but keep pushing forward. It will get easier. It might take you time to learn to focus, but every day that you try, you'll continue to get better at it. Ultimately, this is about *becoming* someone who focuses, which starts with seeing yourself as such. I recommend that you add a few lines to your affirmations about your commitment to unwavering focus and what you will do each day to develop it.

Most college students would be shocked to discover just how little time they spend on truly important, relevant activities each day. Today, or in the next 24 hours, schedule 60 minutes to focus on the *single most important task you do*, and you'll be amazed not only by your productivity, but also by how empowering it feels.

By now, you've added some pretty incredible action items and focus areas to your success arsenal. After you complete the steps below, head into the next section where we will sharpen your Level 10 College Student Success Skills and combine them with the Life S.A.V.E.R.S. in ways you might not have heard or thought of before! Remember the steps we discussed in this chapter on the importance of unwavering focus and the ways to increase it in your life.

PUTTING UNWAVERING FOCUS INTO ACTION

Step One: Choose or create your ideal environment to support unwavering focus. If your focus is optimal when you're working in a public place, schedule focused blocks of time at Starbucks, for example. If you work from home, make sure you've implemented step two, below.

Step Two: Clear your physical and mental clutter. Start by scheduling a half day to clean up your workspace. Then clear your mind with a brain dump. Unload all those little to-do items floating around in your head. Create a master to-do list, either on your computer, in your phone, or in your journal.

Step Three: Protect yourself from interruptions that come from *you* and others. Limit distractions that might pull you away from your intended task (turning off notifications), put your phone on Do Not Disturb mode, and set the expectation for people within your circle of influence that you are unavailable during focused time blocks but will get back to them during predesignated times.

Step Four: Start building your Unwavering Focus lists. Pull out your journal or open a note on your phone or computer, and create the following three lists:

- What do I need to keep doing (or do more of)?
- What do I need to start doing?
- What do I need to stop doing?

Begin jotting down everything that comes to mind. Review your lists and determine which activities can be automated, outsourced, or delegated. How much time do you spend on your top academic and success-producing activities? Repeat this process until you are clear on what your process is, then start time-blocking your days so that you're spending close to 80 percent of your time on tasks that produce results. Delegate the rest.

SECTION III:

LEVEL 10 COLLEGE STUDENT SUCCESS SKILLS

7

EXCEPTIONAL COLLEGE STUDENT SUCCESS SKILL #1:

ACADEMICS

Anyone who has never made a mistake has never tried anything new.
—ALBERT EINSTEIN

Music: "Gonna Fly Now"
—BILL CONTI, from the movie *Rocky*

I remember the moment I ordered five hundred dollars' worth of books in the summer before my freshman year of college (a mistake I would never make again). They all arrived in this big brown box, and sometimes I would take a peek inside one of them. When I saw all the tables and figures inside, I started getting really scared, so I shut the book as quickly as I could, threw it back in the big brown box, and returned my attention to enjoying the last summer before starting college.

I got through high school with A's and B's. I took a lot of honors and a few AP classes (in only one of which I passed the AP exam for credit). Beyond my grades, I had a central belief that I would never go to bed before getting all my work done. I would stay up doing all-nighters, drinking Armenian coffee until the morning. My dad wakes up at 6:00 a.m. to get ready for work. When he walked by my room, he'd recognize that I was still working from the night before. He would just look at me and say, "Natalie, you are *so* ready for college."

From those unhealthy all-nighters, my father's words of confidence, and the education I received in high school, I believed that I was ready for college and whatever obstacles might come my way.

Whether you are about to start college or are a few years into it, you have accomplished so much to get to this moment. You've completed many years of school, which undoubtedly came with many late nights completing homework, the stress of studying for exams, and writing all those papers. You have made it through many highs and lows to get here, and I applaud you. You have also read this far into the book, which means you care about yourself and your success. You have chosen to have a college experience filled with personal growth, and that decision will not only help you create success in college, but will also serve you far beyond your graduation day. Whether you are reading this the summer before you begin college, or in the middle of a stressful week in your junior year, you have picked up this book at the right time.

Before students start college, there is a lot of uneasiness. It's like going into the so-called "Unknown." The transition from being a high school student to being a college student can seem a bit scary. Along with that transition, you are told that, in order to be successful *after* college, you must do well *during* college. Hearing that makes you feel some pressure. In fact, I was nervous and I felt that pressure.

I have been right where you are now. I had so many questions in the months before starting college, and I was not even sure where to begin finding the answers! Who am I? Who do I want to become? What major should I study? Who will I hang out with? What should I do with my major? Where can I find a job? How hard will my classes be? Am I going to like my roommate(s)?

College is an educational experience not only in a classroom, but outside the classroom, too. The transition *can* be difficult at times, and it is important for you to do *your* best in college, not anyone else's version of best. Every moment in college will help you gain awareness of who you are as a student *and* as an individual.

Like your peers, you will spend most of your days going to class, studying, and doing all the other things you need to do as a student. In the process, you will learn more about yourself in areas such as who you are, how you study, and how you respond to stress. Gaining self-awareness will take you to the next level *in every area of your personal and academic life.* The more you know yourself, the more strategically you can face the challenges ahead of you and succeed! Doing your Miracle Morning routine will assist you in developing a greater level of awareness, which will create success for you as a student—and in all your future endeavors.

The first level of awareness is learning what you are getting into when you begin college. Naturally, there are many differences between high school and college:

- **Class Schedule:** In high school, you had a set schedule to be in class for seven hours a day. In college, you get to make your schedule. You get to choose if you want to have an 8 a.m. class or if you want to have classes that meet only once a week. It is all dependent on the availability of the classes you want or need to take.

- **Homework:** In high school, you had a lot of busywork, with homework increasing as you got closer to college. In college, you will not have as much busywork, but it depends on the professor and the class. Most of the time, busywork will be assigned reading. Your homework assignments will be less, but they will take a longer time to complete.

- **Grading:** In high school, your work may have mostly been graded based on completion. If you completed the work, you would receive full credit. Although this may happen in college in some of your classes, most of your assignments will be graded. The important parts of your grades, like papers and exams, will be weighted more heavily for your final grade, while in high school your grades had a blanket of safety with class participation and full-credited homework assignments.

Hal has a saying, "Who you're becoming is far more important than what you're doing, and yet it's what you're doing that determines who you're becoming." College is a place where you get to make decisions and do what you want. Your decisions will dictate who you will be during college, and more importantly, who you will become in the process. In college, you get to choose whether you want to exceed the minimum in your classes or slide by just to pass the class. The saying "C's get degrees" is true. You could get C's in all your classes and still get a degree, but where would that lead you? Is that your idea of success? I know you are here because you have chosen the path to excel rather than just sliding by in college.

ACADEMIC SELF-AWARENESS

During college, there is a wealth of knowledge you are exposed to daily. However many years you have been in college, you are constantly learning about yourself and how you want to use your education for your future. As a student, one of the most important decisions you will make in college is declaring your major. It is a single step that narrows down what your future might be like, who you will spend your time with, and what you spend many hours studying. After choosing your major, it is important to maximize the depth of knowledge within that major and develop yourself in the process.

I got accepted into LMU as a psychology major, but decided during summer orientation not to pursue that major. I was now an undeclared liberal arts major but was also on the pre-health track. I laughed at how truly undecided I was about my life, and I embraced it fully. I recognize now that being undecided at the start of college shaped me into who I am today. I believe it is completely acceptable to be undecided when beginning college, just as long as you have the intention to actively search for what you do want to study or pursue as a career. Choosing your major is an important decision, but part of that is increasing your self-awareness about your grand vision of life, and which major will get you closer to that vision.

Whether you already know which major you are studying or not, here are action steps to take to increase your knowledge of what is possible for you within a major or career:

1. What might you see yourself doing in one year? Three years? Five years?

I believe asking the right questions can help you narrow down what your interests are. Although these questions sound like you may be at an interview with an employer or on a date, it is important to ask these kinds of questions of yourself. What is it that you see yourself doing in the future? Do you see yourself possibly in science labs? Behind a camera? Writing scripts? Conducting research studies?

When you are able to answer one question, ask yourself a follow-up question such as, *Why is this important to me?* The more you learn about yourself and clarify your vision, the better you will be able to make decisions, including choosing a major and how you want to use that major to progress in your academic career.

Your Miracle Morning routine can play a pivotal role here. The morning is the ideal time to reflect about these questions before the rest of the world makes demands on your time and attention. The morning is YOUR time to think about your future, who you are, and who you want to become. By using *silence, affirmations, visualization, exercise, reading,* and *scribing,* you can dive into the mental space needed to step up to the next level in your life. I have a feeling you will be too busy to ask yourself these questions when you have homework to do later that night, right? That is why the morning is the best time. No one will interrupt you in the mornings, and you'll get to use all your energy to learn more about yourself each day.

2. Read Books

I know what you are probably thinking: *"Don't I have enough to read already, Natalie?"* Yes you do. However, this is reading for a different purpose. Books are a magical portal where you can find the answer to any question you have when it comes to majors, goals, and careers. The best part is that there is a book out there for every question you want answered. It is an opportunity to gain knowledge in any area you choose. During your Miracle Morning routine, you can use your *reading* time to learn more about a certain career, which can help you discern whether that field is right for you. Knowledge is power, and the more you know, the better you will be able to make decisions in choosing your major or exploring a career.

3. Try Out Introductory Classes

Trying out the intro-level classes that your college offers can give you many insights. You can sign up for a class and see for yourself whether the subject matter aligns with who you are and your interests.

Let's say you've always loved looking at the stars and you want to learn more about them, so you decide to take an astronomy class that your college offers. You may end up loving the class, OR you may not like it and even drop the class in the first week! What's great is that you can try out a lot of classes during the add/drop period, and you won't be tied down to a class unless you decide to take it. Whatever you choose to do after those first few classes, give yourself a high-five for at least trying something to explore your options. It is far better than not taking that astronomy class and standing on the podium on graduation day thinking, "What if I had liked astronomy?" In this case, it's better to know now than later!

4. Talk to Your Academic Counselor

Academic counselors are great resources who are here to help you narrow down your major, fulfill your degree requirements, and make sure that you are accomplishing your personal academic goals. They have great insight and advice to give about what your next step should be in clarifying your vision.

When I was trying to figure out which major to choose, my academic advisor guided me in the process. She helped me weigh the pros and cons for the majors I was considering. I had to make a decision among biochemistry, chemistry, or environmental science. In the end, she helped me choose chemistry because it would allow me to graduate on time, and it gave me the opportunities to achieve the goals that fit my vision at that time.

5. Talk to Your Professors and Look at Their Research

Professors love it when students are engaged in their classes. They also love it when students ask them questions about their field of study. If you visit your professor's office hours just to ask him what he loved about studying a certain major in college or for grad school, it might help you decide whether or not you like that path for yourself. This is such a productive step to take, because professors were students just like you before they earned their degrees. They have lots of wisdom and knowledge to impart, and they are usually so willing to talk about their academic journey.

When I was a first-year student, I really loved a philosophy class that I took. I talked to the professor about why he thought he wanted to be a professor of philosophy. He said he decided to study philosophy because no other class interested him and he had failed every other subject in college. Although failing every class is hardly a good thing to do, he was able to clearly see what he wanted to spend so much time studying for the entirety of college, and even after college. After that conversation, I was able to recognize that philosophy would not be a good fit for me, and I moved on to the next area of interest that I wanted to explore.

Another step you can take while talking to your professors is asking what they do in their research. It will give you insight into the various topics that could be explored within one major or profession. Before I declared chemistry as my major during my sophomore year, I was always searching on the school's website for what each professor studied; if one of their studies piqued my interest, I would make it a point to set up a meeting with them to discuss their research. The general rule here is: The more you know, the more clearly you can make your own decisions in your academic career.

6. Talk To Your Friends

In college, you will not only learn from your professors, but also from the people you spend all your time with: your friends and classmates. I believe that you can learn something from everyone. Each individual is a piece of knowledge within a large puzzle. My friend Matt Aitchison, host of the podcast *The Millionaire Mindcast*, often says, "I'm a student of life and I'm always looking for my next teacher." Your friends will be taking different classes according to their interests or major. Everyone you meet is taking lower- or upper-division classes of some sort, so there is a lot you can learn from your own peers, and it is a much more informal way of getting that information than talking to professors. You can simply ask them how they like their major or their classes. This is a great way to get to know more about your friends, and learning more about others gives you a greater insight into yourself.

———

If you realize that you are not happy with the major you are studying, do not be afraid to change it. There are many people who change their major multiple times in college. Breathe, you will be okay! Most of the time, you are still able to graduate on time, too. Talk to your guidance counselor or a professor in the major you want to study next to help you with your transition.

Following these steps to gather all the knowledge you need will allow you to declare a major and explore your interests for a clearer vision. It is crucial to take classes that pertain to your field, most especially to complete the prerequisites for graduate programs. For example, if you want to go to graduate school and study theology, then it might just fit for you to study theology during your undergraduate career instead of a foreign language. Another example is if you want to enter into the allied health professions like physical therapy or speech pathology. It is important you talk to an academic counselor so that you are informed of the major that would best meet your prerequisites for graduate programs.

———

Now, what I write next may seem to contradict the message of what I just wrote:

Your major may not equal your profession after college.

Conan O'Brien, host of *Conan* on TBS, has a degree in history and American literature from Harvard. He graduated Magna Cum Laude, and now he is the host of his own late-night TV show! Actress Eva Longoria has a degree in kinesiology from Texas A&M University-Kingsville. Lisa Kudrow, beloved cast member on the show *Friends*, has a degree in accounting from Vassar College. Mayim Bialik, actress in the hit show *Big Bang Theory*, has a Ph.D. in Neuroscience from UCLA. Comedy icon Will Ferrell has a degree in sports information from the University of Southern California. Rowan Atkinson, the actor famously known for the character Mr. Bean, has a degree in electrical engineering from Newcastle University, and also has a master's degree from Oxford.

I would like to add that this very book you are reading is written by someone who has a bachelor's degree in chemistry, not in English or psychology! Here's the point: You do not know how you will change as you gain greater self-awareness during your time in college, and life has a way of taking turns you didn't expect. What is important for you is to go ahead and make the best decision you can right now. Be confident on your path to success!

As a student, one of the most important parts of your academic life is going to class. Some classes will have exciting lectures and some classes will bore you out of your mind, but you have to do what you have to do to graduate and perform well.

Besides studying, here are five action steps to take so you can do well and be confident in your classes:

1. Always Show Up

Unless you have a valid excuse—you're really sick or you have a life-altering interview that could not be scheduled for any other time—you NEED to go to class. If you want to at least pass your classes without doing any other work, you NEED to go to class. There will be days when you will not want to go to class. Your bed will look so inviting, and you'll just want to catch up on your favorite shows on Netflix, but you should go to class anyway. If you are someone who likes to skip class, you will inevitably miss information and have a hard time passing the class.

By not going to class, you will be wasting much more time than you might believe, because you will spend a lot of time after that class trying to figure out what you missed. Even if you have a friend who can take notes for you, you probably will not be able to understand their notes because they take notes in a way that matches how they understand the material, not how you will understand the material. To say it simply: Skipping class is not worth it. Go to class, because a large part of success is just showing up.

2. Come Prepared

Coming prepared does not mean to make sure you have your pen and notebook in your backpack (although you definitely should). What I mean is to come mentally and intellectually prepared.

For instance, I have a good friend named Taylor who is one of the most kind and intelligent people I have ever met in my life. But while walking to class, she is so focused that she does not recognize her friends who are walking right past her, waving their hands trying to grab her attention. She has extreme focus. She already knows what concept the professor will be teaching in class and has her questions ready from the start. Because she is prepared, she knows how to structure her notes to help her later when she has to study for her exams. She and I took the same classes, and when I compared my notes with hers, I would end up using her notes to study because they were so much better than mine.

I am not saying that you need to be as focused as Taylor before your classes. Definitely wave back to your friends who are trying to say hello! But do take some time before you walk to class to look over what the professor will be covering in class. Your Miracle Morning is a great time to review class material before your classes that day. Even if you do not understand everything you're reading, try to read through it anyway. That way, you can enter class with a greater context for what your professor is going to be discussing, and it will be your second time hearing the material instead of the first. This can make all the difference for how well you do on your exams in that class.

3. Take Good Notes

The notes you take during class will help you when it comes time for your midterms or final exams. Unfortunately, most students realize they have not taken great notes when they are reviewing them for exams. Make sure that you look back at your notes often so that you understand everything you wrote. You can even ask your professor how to take the best notes for the way they teach their class.

Some classes may be different in terms of which ways would be most effective for taking notes, which is why I think it is important to talk to your professor. There are so many different teaching styles and so much different subject matter that you need to be able to adjust with the class and stay alert for the best way to capture its information. You will surely thank yourself when you have notes that spell out the concepts clearly when studying for your midterms and final exams.

A great resource to find effective ways to study and do well during college is College Info Geek created by Thomas Frank. His website, collegeinfogeek.com, has great articles and videos to teach you effective study methods so you can do well in your classes and land your dream job after college.

4. Visit Your Professors' Office Hours

There are numerous benefits to visiting your professor's office hours. During my first year when I was taking chemistry classes, I never understood the topics that were being taught in class. I would always be afraid to go to my professors' office hours because I did not want them to think that I was not trying to understand the material.

Here is the reality with office hours: Your professors wait in their offices, sometimes with no one showing up, and they are waiting to help their students. They want students to come in! It is important to go to office hours, even if you do not know what questions to ask. Any important concept that they can teach you one-on-one can help you learn more easily. Understanding that one concept will help you with understanding the rest of the topic, too. Whether or not you want to go to office hours, it is best to go anyway. Your teachers will recognize your effort to do well in their classes.

An additional benefit is that students who attend office hours often might get a bump up in their letter grade. I was always told that, at the end of a class, the professor would bump a student's grade from a B+ to an A- only if they had consistently shown up at their office hours. Other students who were on the border of two letter grades would not get a bump up in their grades if they did not attend office hours.

On a different note, I highly recommend visiting your professors' office hours during the first week simply to introduce yourself. In a class of 50–300+ students, you will now stand out as someone who cares about the professor and the class, they will know your name, and they will be more than willing to help you during the quarter or semester.

5. Utilize School Resources

Colleges and universities have so many free resources, yet many students do not take advantage of them. There is no shame in needing or asking for help. It only means that you want to improve and are taking action for yourself, which some people do not do.

There are usually tutoring services, writing services, a health center, psychological services, library databases, career counseling services, and spirituality services on your campus ready for you to use them! A college campus is the perfect place to get all the help you need to succeed as a student and as an individual! If you are a student with a disability, make sure to utilize Student Disability Support Services (SDSS) as well. They are there to help you. I recently learned that SDSS can also be used by students who do not have a documented disability. They can give students extensions on tests if there is a good enough reason to. However, if you need an extension, I recommend talking to your professor as soon as you know you need an extension. They are usually accommodating if your reason is valid.

Now that we have gone over ways to do well in your classes, know that it does take work to do well in them. Some classes may be easier than others, but as you progress in your chosen majors, your classes will increase in difficulty. This difficulty will serve to help mold you into the person you want to become at the end of college.

BEATING PROCRASTINATION

Although I may have told you what you have to do to succeed in your classes, there is a negative tendency most students (including myself) have that does not serve them. It's called procrastination. Ever heard of it? I am certain you have, and I am 100% positive that you have procrastinated at least once by this point in your life. In high school, I was the "Queen of Procrastination." Over time, my friends just assumed I stayed up all night to do work and did not sleep. I always left my homework to the last minute, but also always made sure I finished my work.

It took me too many years to learn that putting things off until the last minute is not the best thing for me to do. Students fall behind on their work because there is so much going on in any given day. However, let's be honest, we all procrastinate even when we have the time to do an assignment. I'm guessing you'll deal with your procrastination problem … tomorrow? Nope! Not this time. We are going to conquer it today, right now.

Before learning how to overcome procrastination, you must know why people procrastinate. By recognizing the reason(s) why you procrastinate, you can grow your awareness and solve the problem at its source before you let procrastination stop you from accomplishing your goals. According to a MotivationGrid post titled "4 Main Causes of Procrastination Revealed," the four causes of procrastination are (1) Fear of Failure, (2) Excessive Perfectionism, (3) Low Energy Levels, and (4) Lack of Focus. Let's dive into each of these causes of procrastination and their respective solutions.

1. Fear of Failure:

It is not necessarily the failing itself that people are afraid of, but rather the consequences of failure. People ask themselves, *What's going to happen if I fail?* Students are particularly afraid of failing because it will be catastrophic to their GPA, which may affect their chances of getting a job they want after graduation or getting accepted into a graduate program. This is completely understandable; however, the fear of failure is really preventing you from growing into the person you desire to become. Failure builds character and awareness, which are what most employers and graduate schools really look for now. Keep in mind, too, that the word "failure" is skewed in the academic sphere, because it pertains to literally failing—earning an "F"— in a class and how that leads to decreased chances of success after graduation. I choose not to use the word *failure* in my vocabulary anymore; I switched it out for the word *lesson.*

Solution: Recognize that failure, especially in your classes, is not the end. College is actually the best time to "fail," because the only thing it will affect is one grade on your transcript. There is nothing to fear because in your life, you cannot fail. You only learn, grow, and become better than you've ever been before. You get to choose the way you perceive and use your *lesson.* Keep working and put your fear at bay; it has no use for your growth. You also cannot avoid failure. It happens to everybody, so you might as well keep working hard toward your goals. *When* you "fail," use it to empower you into the best version of yourself. Also, you failed because it means you tried something, and that is always better than not trying at all. You never fail, you only learn.

2. Excessive Perfectionism:

What usually happens is that people are not able to attack an obstacle if they believe they cannot do it with perfection. Students can become paralyzed looking at an assignment knowing that they will not be able to do it well, which causes them not to try at all. In college, nothing will be perfect, because you are still learning and growing. You can try your best, but expecting perfection from yourself will always cause you to feel inadequate, and that is exactly the opposite of what you are.

Solution: Be content with *completion*. There is a lot of time and mental energy wasted in reaching for perfection. Make sure you try to do your best, but be happy with what you have completed. Completing an assignment, even if it is not absolutely perfect, will always be better than having a perfect but incomplete assignment.

3. Low Energy Levels:

When people do not have the energy, then they physically cannot accomplish their goals. It is like trying to work a car without fuel in the gas tank. As a college student, taking care of your energy is one of the most important things that will determine your success—which is why we spent so much time discussing energy engineering in chapter 5. A lack of energy due to imbalance in your health affects every other part of your life, too.

Solution: Make sure you are figuring out the right amount of sleep, types of food, and exercise routine *you* need that will give you long-lasting energy. Every person is different in this regard. Some people need 8 hours of sleep, while some can thrive on 6 hours. Make sure you are eating nutrient-rich foods that can help you remain strong and healthy for the duration of college. When it comes to exercise, you have to do it so you can remain in an optimum state during your studies. If you do not exercise, it is like keeping your car sitting in the garage and never taking it for a drive: The car will not drive to its full capability. Who wouldn't want a car to function smoothly? (You can thank my father for the car metaphors.)

4. Lack of Focus:

When someone does not know themselves well, or does not have a strong reason to do work, then there is no reason for them to focus or achieve any goals. This is a common occurrence for college students, especially when their work can become overwhelming at times and they have not figured out what to make of their time in college.

Solution: Whether or not you have found a reason that helps you focus and complete your tasks, it is important to strive for self-improvement. There will be moments in your life that will call for you to step up to difficult challenges, and you will be able to conquer those based on your improvement as a student and as an individual. Set some realistic goals for yourself that will inspire you and that you can accomplish with a greater effort. This will allow you to grow and remain inspired for future goals.

Additional Solution: A life purpose isn't something you find. It doesn't come to you in a dream and is not written in the sky for you to decipher. **You get to create your life purpose, whatever it is that you want it to be.** Write down a life purpose that you can see every day as a reminder of why the work you are doing is worth doing. A life purpose that empowers me to do my work is: "My success gives others the permission to do the same." It is taken partially from the famous Marianne Williamson passage quoted earlier in this book. I want every one of my friends and family to improve in their own lives. If they can see that I am growing each day, then they will believe that they are capable of improving themselves, too.

Did one or more of those causes of procrastination resonate with you? All four of them resonated with me during college. It is important for you to identify what is causing you to procrastinate. This will allow you to overcome your procrastination. It is important that you immediately do what it takes to take you out of the mental space that causes you to procrastinate and get back on the road of growth. Do not blame yourself if your brain goes back into a disempowered mindset; it is just like a muscle, and you have to train it to bring you back into the present so you can get your work done. You will develop the strength you need over time and you will notice that the frequency of your procrastination will decrease. Something that helped me was that when I hustled and did most of my work during the day while the sun was out, I got lots of work done, and I was a happier person. After a day's work, I would only have a few assignments left by nightfall, rather than having to starting everything late at night.

When it comes to your academics and your health, time is precious. You need to make sure to maximize your time during the day so that you will limit those long nights that will throw you off balance. Managing your time with your priorities and goals is so important. Here are time-management tips that will take you from an unorganized student to an organized student:

1. Write out your to-do list, with due dates for each task.

2. Separate your tasks by groups to prioritize your responsibilities. Group A is Highest Priority; Group B is a Definite Priority; Group C is Lowest Priority. The rule of thumb is that if you do not complete Group A tasks, you do not move on to Group B tasks.

3. Create a timeline by writing your tasks down in order of what needs to be completed first, second, and so on.

4. Write down the dates of these time-dependent tasks in your schedule.

5. Work it all out during your Miracle Morning! You can make sure to achieve one of your priorities during your Miracle Morning routine, which will put you on track to accomplish your goals.

6. Find an accountability partner to keep you on course even if you begin to slack off. Share with them the tasks you have to complete and their completion dates so that you accomplish your tasks and succeed! Be an accountability partner back by keeping your friend accountable for their goals, too.

A planner that helps me manage my time, put procrastination at bay, and succeed during college is the Passion Planner. I love that the daily time schedule is from 6:00 a.m. to 10:30 p.m. with 30-minute increments, which is realistic for college student scheduling. It also has sections for brainstorming ideas and ranking your personal and work priorities so you can clearly identify what you need to do first. You can even get it as a free printable PDF! You can find out how to do that at www.passionplanner.com. Alongside the Passion Planner, the Self Control program on my computer is also very useful to minimize procrastination. It is an application that allows you to block out all the websites you would usually use to procrastinate for any range from 5 minutes to 24 hours. During the most difficult weeks of college, this application helped me remain focused and get my work done.

I have given you lots of information to increase your academic self-awareness, succeed in your classes, overcome procrastination, and manage your time, but I want to leave you with a story that I hope inspires you to overcome your procrastination and achieve your goals.

Jeff Hoffman, CEO of Priceline.com, says: "Your success is someone else's miracle." I could not agree more. After finding out I was going to coauthor this book, one of my younger cousins who is eight years old would ask me often how my book was coming along. I would talk to him about how there is a lot of work to be done, but how happy I was to be doing it all. Months later, he showed me a piece of paper of his mini-vision board. On it he wrote, "I want to be an auther." I broke down into tears because in that moment I realized that I helped my younger cousin to dream a bigger dream. I absolutely loved how he spelled "auther" too, a sweet moment I will cherish forever. I cannot wait until I help him write his first book.

Every time you "fail" and pick yourself up afterwards, you give someone the courage to do the same. Whether you believe it or not, your success does influence those who know you and even those who don't, so keep going and do not give up.

Although there will always be work to do, there will always be some play, too! Let's use this momentum to dive right into the next chapter about your next Level 10 College Student Area: your social life.

8

EXCEPTIONAL COLLEGE STUDENT SUCCESS
SKILL #2:

SOCIAL LIFE

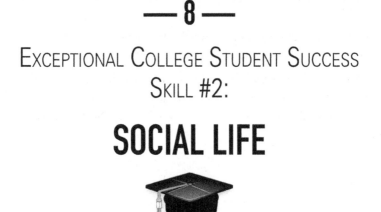

Kindness is the language which the deaf can hear and the blind can see.
—MARK TWAIN

We make a living by what we get. We make a life by what we give.
—WINSTON CHURCHILL

Music: "You've Got a Friend in Me"
—RANDY NEWMAN, from the movie *Toy Story*

Move over, academics. The best thing about college is the experiences you will have with the people you meet. During your first year, you may know only a few people from orientation or maybe no one at all, and that is completely normal. Through your time in college, you will meet people with whom you will always have a great time, people who will inspire you and change you as a person, and ones you will keep as friends forever.

Whether you are an introvert or extrovert, you will get to meet people in your day-to-day activities in class, the coffee shop, the cafeteria, and even while walking around. Most college students yearn to find a place at college where they feel at home. In order to find your place during college, you will have to get out of your comfort zone, which might make you uneasy at first. It helps to know that everyone is feeling the same way, too. Stepping outside of your comfort zone will allow you to explore who you are and meet people to form deep and meaningful friendships.

Besides meeting people through regular day-to-day college activities, here are six different avenues to become more socially engaged with your peers on campus:

1. Join a Club

On every college campus, there are many clubs that you can join. There are academic clubs, entertainment clubs, club sports, cultural clubs, Greek Life organizations, professional clubs, recreation clubs, religious/spiritual clubs, political clubs, service and social justice clubs.

Joining clubs on campus is easy, and it will lead to growth in your personal life, too. At LMU, there is a Harry Potter club, ice skating club, Ultimate Frisbee club, and so many other awesome ones! By joining groups like these, you get to meet people who have similar interests. You are bound to meet people you like at club meetings, and club activities will keep introducing you to more people.

2. Create Your Own Club

What if you don't see a club that interests you? Create your own! Chances are, other people would want to join you in your endeavor. Starting a club can also be a way to leave a legacy on campus. Some friends who I met my first year in college created the Ultimate Frisbee club that I listed above. Four friends teamed up during their sophomore year and started meeting each week to play Ultimate Frisbee; it is still one of the most popular clubs on campus. A simple idea not only brought people together, but also created leadership positions that each of the founders could learn and grow from. These kinds of experiences will give you skills you need to succeed after college—a win-win from every angle.

In 2013 while attending American Jewish University, college student Brianna Greenspan, who later became the coauthor of *The Miracle Morning Art of Affirmations: A Positive Coloring Book for Adults and Kids*, created the first ever Miracle Morning club in the nation. In 2016, my good friends Michele and Erin Matsuoka created a Miracle Morning club at Poway High School in San Diego. There are many Miracle Morning hangouts all over the country, and there is a huge opportunity to create Miracle Morning clubs on your college campus!

Having a group of positive people committed to improving their lives who practice the Miracle Morning can be so beneficial for everyone in that group—and important for your personal development. It creates a support system you can lean on during your time in school. Also, it's especially powerful when you all can physically come together on campus, rather than just meeting over social media. Everyone in the club can find accountability partners, too, which will ensure that you all succeed in your personal and academic goals.

You can also create a Miracle Morning community within your residence hall! Talk to your RA about offering programs connected to the concepts of the Miracle Morning. In doing so, you can design an environment of peace and support for your friends, roommates, and classmates. Your meetings could include doing the Life S.A.V.E.R.S. together, or you could start a book club or sign up for marathons and train together! I can picture you now, forming the greatest friendships within this club. Reach out to The Miracle Morning for College Students Facebook community for help on how to set it all up and to get creative ideas for what activities you can do as a club.

3. Volunteer

Gaining volunteer experience during college will teach you a lot about yourself and help you realize the fulfillment that comes from giving your time and energy to others.

During my sophomore year, I was accepted into an on-campus group called the Gryphon Circle Service Organization. It is an all-female club with a focus on education. I had to complete a certain number of volunteer hours per semester at a service site, and I chose to volunteer at a convalescent home. That was an incredible opportunity to be of service to others who needed help, and it was also a great growth experience for me.

The people who you spend the most time with will be a reflection of who you are and who you want to become. (See the next section of this chapter for more on this concept.) The women of this organization put aside time each week to visit their service sites and give back to others in the community surrounding LMU. Each week, I spent time with these women learning and growing with each other at each group meeting. As an organization, we had intentional conversations about how to best serve marginalized communities in the Los Angeles area. It is because of the women in Gryphon Circle and my experiences as a member of the service organization that I realized that I wanted to be a voice for college students.

4. Become a Student Leader

There are so many ways you can gain a leadership role on your campus. You can run for student government, join the resident housing association, or work for the student services office. You will learn a lot about how to lead, meet, and work with many passionate people. During my college career, I was very involved with helping first-year students as an orientation leader and resident advisor, and in other jobs I had within the student services department. Through this work, I was able to gain a lot of information about LMU that was useful to me personally, and I got to help people who needed resources on campus or my advice. Being a leader was one of the highlights of my college career. Through these leadership positions, I was able to learn about what students need and how I could help them. I also learned to analyze and solve different problems, and I built relationships with others who share my passion for helping students.

Taking on a leadership position can be time-consuming. Make sure that you are passionate about the position, and be sure it works alongside your other commitments. See how much room you have left in your schedule after you spend time on academics, with friends, and taking care of your health. If you can dedicate the time to be a leader on campus and you really want to do it, go for it—it's a very rewarding experience.

5. Pursue International Experience

Mark Twain described traveling best: "Travel is fatal to prejudice, bigotry, and narrow-mindedness, and many of our people need it sorely on these accounts. Broad, wholesome, charitable views of men and things cannot be acquired by vegetating in one little corner of the earth all one's lifetime."

During college, you will have opportunities to travel. You can go on service trips or study abroad. Whether the trip is for only one week or lasts a whole year, investing in an international experience is one of the greatest opportunities you can take for yourself, and you'll meet amazing people who will share the experience with you.

International experience is an opportunity to learn about other cultures, patterns of living, and values. It will give you greater insight into your own culture, too. It opens your mind to the way others live. It expands your own thoughts of what is possible for you.

If you choose to study abroad, you will travel and continue your academic studies at the same time. Even though it might be scary to live in a foreign country, it is one of the greatest experiences you can have, and most people have this opportunity only while they're in college. You will have to get your homework done, but when I studied abroad I found that my friends and I wanted to hang out all the time, so we made sure we got our work done as quickly as we could!

Until I spent four months studying abroad in Bonn, Germany, I never believed that I wanted to be away from the beautiful LMU campus or my family for so long. I felt as though I would have missed out on something at home. What I found out soon after arriving in Germany, however, was that if I had not studied abroad, I would have missed out an even more amazing experience. I was still a full-time student, but on the weekends my friends and I would hang out all over town or travel to neighboring European countries.

Although traveling within Europe was wonderful, it was not the most significant part of my time studying abroad. What was more important was learning how to do everything on my own, gaining independence, and becoming confident in myself. During the four months I was in Germany, I grew so much as a person, and realized there was a lot I could accomplish through my own might and will. It was exactly what I needed after a year of struggling with my mental health.

My friends and I studied and traveled together, and the experiences we shared have kept us strongly connected even after graduation. Studying abroad helped me realize that there was a lot to life beyond academics and grades. There were dreams to be accomplished, and a beautiful life to be designed.

One special thing about my study abroad experience is that I brought *The Miracle Morning* with me and read it while traveling all over Europe. Soon after that I started my routine, and it has been my life's greatest adventure since!

After my experience abroad, I recognized how much I love to travel, and that I want to take a vacation at least once every year. I am ready to work hard to accomplish that dream and make it a reality! The desire to travel is now a big motivation factor for me. In this one life that I have, I am going to make sure I travel all over the world.

If you have the chance to study abroad or pursue any other type of international experience, take the opportunity. Not only will you meet great people and see new parts of the world, you will also gain inner confidence about what you are capable of! Make sure to ask your school about scholarships and grants that you can apply for, like the Charles A. Gibson Scholarship, which is specifically for studying abroad.

6. Land an Internship or Job

By searching around, you can find fun internships and jobs, where you will definitely meet people who have similar interests. It's in your best interest to get involved with work that gives you greater knowledge about your potential field; you'll be able to see different possible career paths and be exposed to different working environments.

You will learn from your coworkers how they feel about working in that particular field, and how it may have changed over the years. Beyond that, you might also meet people you'll work with later in your career! Often, students who do well in their internships are given full-time positions with the same organizations after college. So while you are meeting people within your potential future career, you are also gaining hands-on experience and increasing your chances of being employed after college.

I hope you recognize now that you are going to meet A LOT of people during your time in college. Creating connections with others brings the opportunity for meaningful relationships that will remain strong even after college.

AVERAGE OF YOUR FIVE FRIENDS

Although you will meet a lot of people in college, here is something you should remember: "You are the average of the five friends you spend the most time with." This Jim Rohn quote might be one of the most important things you learn from this book.

Have you noticed that you are somewhat similar to your closest friends? You might listen to the same music or like the same shows. Surprisingly, it works the same way with everything else, too. If the five people you spend the most time with in college are always complaining and do not care about school, then you should expect to become someone who complains a lot and doesn't care about school, either. The converse is also true: If you surround yourself with people who are intelligent, hard-working, and genuinely kind and happy people, then you will become like them, too.

Are you hanging out with the people you want to become?

Right now, take out a piece of paper (I'll wait ...) and take ten minutes to truly evaluate the people you spend the most time with in your life. Do your friends push you to be better, or to be mediocre? Do they inspire you, or do they drain all the energy out of you? Do your friends take care of their health, or do they make that their last priority?

If your friends complain a lot and leave you feeling hopeless, agitated, or angry, then you need to upgrade your friend circle as quickly as you can. The longer you surround yourself with them, the more you will become like them. In this transition, please do not simply ignore your previous friends completely and leave them in the dark about why you are not talking to them anymore. Have the courage to tell them in person (not via text message) about how they make you feel and why you cannot be friends with them. You will be doing them a favor, because they may have never realized that they make you feel that way, and it's important for them to know. Once they do know, they might want to improve themselves. Maybe they're simply unaware of their impact, and you can bring that awareness into their lives. If they don't understand, or don't take well what you are telling them, then at least they know why you won't be hanging out with them anymore.

I am going to flip the script on you now. Do *you* complain a lot? Talk badly about others? Watch a lot of TV to avoid what you need to do? Take a look in the mirror and be honest with yourself. This is the time to grow your awareness of how you live your life and what your role is in your friend group. If you find that you are the negative person, be proud of yourself for owning up to it. You might just be in a negative place in your life right now. I myself had negative tendencies that used to stunt my personal growth and made me a bad friend. What is important is that you identify the areas you need to work on to be a better person, because your disempowered actions affect not only you, but also your friends. By improving yourself, you are improving the friend you can be to others who need you. If you are not sure of your role in a group, do what I did and ask your friends,

"How can I be a better friend to you?" By putting that on the table, you are creating the opportunity for your own growth.

If you find out that you are *that* person in the group, do not be hard on yourself. You were not aware, but then you took steps to increase your awareness. When you become your best self, you inspire others to be better people, too. Be proud that you took that step for yourself! This is a moment for celebration!

LIVE LIFE IN THE FRONT ROW

Alongside the concept that "You are the average of the five friends you spend the most time with," I ask you to live life in the front row. What does that mean? Let me explain.

The Front Row Foundation is a charity co-founded by Jon Vroman. This foundation gives front row experiences to those who are terminally ill and facing critical health conditions. Participants get a chance to see their favorite band or sports team up close! It is a moment they get to share with their family, and it becomes a favorite memory they can replay in their minds for the rest of their lives. If you have ever been to a concert of your favorite band or a big game for your favorite team, haven't you thought, "Man, I wish I was sitting right there in the front row!" We know life is so much better in the front row: Everyone is having the time of their lives. The front row is where you get to experience all of life's energy and passion!

I was listening to an episode of one of my favorite podcasts, *The Millionaire Mindcast*, in which the host, Matt Aitchison, had Jon Vroman on as a guest. During that episode, Jon talked about what it means to live life in the front row. It means "getting close to the things, the people, and the thoughts that inspire you and make you feel alive"—experiencing all the amazing things your life has to offer. Not only should you live your life in the front row, but you should also be a maker of *front row moments* for yourself and others. When was the last time you did something that made you feel courageous? Where you feel like you stepped up? When did you feel you were fully engaged in an activity—in *flow*? When was the last time you felt transformed? When was the last time you knew that what you did created a connection with others? These kinds of qualities make up front row moments.

In the hustle and bustle of college, it is important that you do not get caught up in all the little things that can overwhelm you. Living life in the front row means that you are present with all the good that is around you instead. It is about creating intentional connections with others, and making sure to create an atmosphere of love and support.

As explained earlier, the people you surround yourself with determine the quality of the life you live. To live life in the front row, it is important to identify who you would want in *your* front row. If you were doing a speech on a big stage in front of a large audience, who would you want cheering you on from the front row? Whose smiles would you want to see there? Write a list of five to eight people, the ones who always support you and want to make your dreams come true. You can create different lists for different aspects of your life such as academics, spirituality, work, etc. When you come up with your list, tell those people on your list that they are in your front row, and how special that is for you. Thank them for having such a positive influence on your life.

Living life in the front row means you need to make sure you are there for others, most especially those you care about the most. Make sure that you ask the people you love what their dreams are, and how you can support them to help them live their dreams. The quality of the relationships you develop with others is a reflection of who you are and the value you want to give to others. By living life in the front row, you give yourself permission to succeed and to be a reason others succeed, too. One of my favorite quotes from Hal is: "It's okay to be average, as long as you surround yourself with extraordinary people that you become the average of." You will feel the change very quickly once your social circle is filled with the best people you know.

SOCIAL MEDIA

Besides meeting people through clubs, work, classes, or your other involvements, a large part of our social life has become connected with social media. Whether you're on Facebook, Twitter, Instagram, Snapchat, or LinkedIn, each day that you are on it, you are connecting with friends about the content they post. Social media has become something students automatically do between classes, as a break from their homework (*cough* procrastination), and as a way to show others what they are up to that day. It is a great way to connect with people you do not see often if they live far away, and it is also a great form of communication for clubs and organizations on campus. Whether you like it or not, social media has become a necessary tool for connecting with your peers.

Your social media feed, however, also has everything to do with whether you are improving as a person. It's true! Sometimes our feeds can be filled with lots of negativity. Do your friends use their social media platforms to complain a lot? Many people use social media as an outlet for their stresses and frustrations with their own lives. They use it as a platform to be seen and heard when things are hard. I realized this during my senior year of college, when a lot of the posts and pictures that I was seeing were negative. Behind each message, there was someone who complained about their life and did not realize that they have the power to change anything in their life. I saw a lot of pictures that placed false expectations on what life really is like.

When I noticed this, I made a decision to fill my social media feeds with posts from people who make me think, that are rooted in love, and that remind me of lessons I learned a long time ago and what I am grateful for in my life. Usually, those kinds of posts are from people who have helped me in my life, who have added value by giving advice about how to become healthier or happier.

What I realized is that the posts we see on our news feeds are what our subconscious reflects into our lives. When I saw a negative post, my mind felt disempowered. There are posts that can be "perfect," too, which does not serve anyone, either. As students, whether you are doing homework or in the middle of chemistry lab, you'll have those days when you dream about being somewhere enchanting and beautiful where you can be careless and stress-free. In the most stressful and anxiety-filled days of my college career, I used to see pictures on social media of people living "perfect" lives—lying on the beach, sipping on a nutritious smoothie, staring at the bright blue ocean—while I was stressing out about two exams and a paper I had to complete by tomorrow. It created sadness and anxiety in me. It made me question why I was so stressed out at school and why I could not be on the beach having fun. Those kinds of thoughts created additional resistance to achieving my goals, which is not productive for a student's mindset.

In the hardest of times, we fail to remember that people only post the good things about their lives on their social media pages. What they reveal to others online is an incomplete version of their lives. Yes, filters can make pictures look cool sometimes; even I love using filters on my pictures. I am now fully aware, however, that nothing in this world is perfect. The world is not perfect. No student's life is perfect. No one's post-graduation life is perfect. Even the people you admire the most do not live perfect lives. Everyone has an area of their life that they want to improve. It takes hard work to achieve your goals. Do not lose sight of that.

In order for me not to be discouraged, I chose to hide posts from people that were not positively serving my mind, or if they were only spreading negativity into the minds of others (even if they were not aware of it). On another note, if people "unfollow" you on social media, they did you a favor. I began to follow pages that gave posts of positivity and wisdom that could help me. If I was going to procrastinate by checking my Facebook or Instagram, then I was going to consume content that was going to help me succeed, as opposed to consuming content that was going to hurt my psyche.

AN AUTHENTIC REVOLUTION

You will meet many people during the years you are in college. Make sure that the people you surround yourself with are extraordinary, just as you are. *Finding your place* is about finding those friends you want around you. Build your community, your front row, who will support you in your dreams. Be the friend who supports others with their dreams, too. Work together, learn together, laugh together, and grow together. Live that awesome college life of yours alongside the greatest people you will ever meet.

I hope that in our generation, we can arise from the "perfection" that clouds expectations of what life should be like as opposed to what it is. There will be times in college when you won't wash your hair for three days and you order Dominoes for dinner four nights in a row and you eat far too many desserts all at once. This is college! But as long as we remain authentic about the struggles of our experiences during college, we can help others have the freedom to act as their true selves. I have been guilty of being inauthentic on social media, and now I choose to provide value to my followers and make sure that I can help someone solely by my words. By being authentic with your experiences, people will fall in love with you. Showing your vulnerability to others will help others be vulnerable to their friends, too. In this way, we can create healthier and honest atmospheres on college campuses.

Keep being you. You are enough. The Miracle Morning for College Students Facebook community page is the place where you can be transparent with your life and share your struggles and triumphs. Join this community of students who support each other. Let's help each other reach our dreams!

With the right people around you, you now must ensure that you take care of your health so you are able to work toward your dreams, and support your friends in reaching their dreams, too.

Let's get right into how you can achieve Level 10 College Student Health!

— 9 —

EXCEPTIONAL COLLEGE STUDENT SUCCESS SKILL #3:

HEALTH

*The body heals with play, the mind heals with laughter,
and the spirit heals with joy.*

—PROVERB

**Music: "Grateful" by Brotha James
& "Don't Be So Hard on Yourself" by Jess Glynne**

When students start college, the academic environment often causes them to put their work above their health. On a given night, they might sleep only a few hours and wake up feeling exhausted. That causes them to make poor health decisions, such as eating foods that are not nutrient-rich. Then they drink too much coffee so they can have more energy, causing poor quality of sleep, and the cycle starts all over again.

I fell into this trap many times myself. During college, it was really discouraging for me to see my peers sleep more because they were able to get more done during the day. I had to stay up and do all-nighters because I did not know how to prioritize my time. I gave my health lowest priority during college, which over the course of four years caused me to gain 30 pounds, be depressed, and have anxiety. I really wanted to give up on school. I failed some classes along the way that I then had to retake, and I can assure you that retaking chemistry classes is not the most fun thing in the world.

It took me some time to get back on my feet, and the journey to prioritizing my health first was absolutely worth it. Most people stop taking care of themselves when there is a lot they need to get done, yet the more work you have to do, the more you should tending to your health. Even when it is around midterms or finals, there is always *something* you can do to maintain your health. Your health is what allows you to do good work, and should be treated as such. Your body takes care of you. If you do not take care of it, then you will never reach your maximum potential academically or, more importantly, personally.

When it comes to taking care of your health, it is just like your academics: You will get better at it over time. Nothing remains constant in college. Whether it is the difficulty of your classes, your schedule, or the amount of work you have to do, something is always changing. Amid the instability of the college environment, it is important for you to find the ways to best promote your health.

In this chapter, I will give you some tips on how to take care of your health, even when you have a million things to do. Doing so is the most important factor for your well-being as a student and as an individual. When you shift your priorities and place health at #1, your body thanks you by helping you achieve more.

Health is a sum of four components: physical, mental/emotional, environmental, and spiritual. College is a time to build positive habits for yourself, and taking care of your health is arguably the most important positive habit that you can cultivate during college. Quite literally, your health will remain with you for the rest of your life.

PHYSICAL HEALTH

In chapter 5, you read about energy engineering and its importance when it comes to your eating, drinking, and sleeping habits. That information was so important in improving my health. In my first few years of college I definitely ate foods based on their taste. When I was stressed, I usually reached for unhealthy food rather than something that was healthy. I used to have lots of crackers, chips, and chocolate in my room for when I was stressed. I loved eating all of those; however, I became aware of how my energy got depleted after eating those kinds of food. They made me feel groggy.

As my class load increased, I realized that I needed more energy to keep going. I found that eating veggie-rich salads made me feel amazing. I would go to the cafeteria and create my own salad with a bunch of toppings. As a student majoring in chemistry, I used to have to enter four-hour long labs, throughout which I had to feel satiated and alert so I could complete the assigned experiment. Keeping healthy snacks in my backpack and eating nutrient-rich meals like salads made me understand the concept of energy engineering. I even switched out the snacks in my room (except for the chocolate) to lots of fruits and veggies so that when I was stressed, I would reach for the healthier foods rather than ones that would sap my energy.

Just as important as eating nutrient-dense foods is increasing your level of physical activity. In high school, you may have been involved in sports like track and field, cross-country, basketball, or softball, or other activities like the dance club. Practices were always set, so you never had to schedule when you were going to exercise. That all changes in college: Unless you are a student-athlete, no one is going to tell you when to exercise. A lot of times, students forget to plan exercise in their schedule, but you should consider exercise like a class you need to attend as a gift to yourself.

As a college student, you will be spending most of your time sitting down, whether in class, in your room, or in the library as you spend hours writing research papers, studying for exams, and completing other assignments. That's a lot time for your body to be in a sedentary state! It is important for you to give your body the activity that it needs to thrive. By taking study breaks to do some yoga, stretch, or go to a gym class, you can give your body the opportunity to rejuvenate and give you energy in return. You can replenish yourself with 15 minutes of exercise, then head back into your next hour of work. (The most productive students are ones who consistently take planned study breaks.) You will be happy that you did something to take care of your health, even if it was for a short amount of time. Perhaps getting a Fitbit can also be helpful, because it will track your activity and sleep so you can consciously break up your sedentary time.

Besides its ability to help control weight, exercising improves your mood, which boosts your energy and promotes a better quality of sleep. So not only will you be happier, but you will actually *gain* energy from exercising AND sleeping better. When you sleep well, you wake up feeling on top of the world, and you start your day on the right track! Exercising will help you gain productivity in achieving your personal and academic goals. You'll feel good and ready to take your responsibilities head on. Exercise seems like a gift that just keeps on giving.

You might still be thinking, *Natalie, this all sounds amazing, but I don't have time to finish my own work, let alone go to the gym.* I totally get it. I have been there. That's why the Miracle Morning routine is so important. In the *E* portion of the Life S.A.V.E.R.S., you have an opportunity to get your physical state awake and ready to go for the day. Even if you have only 6 minutes, you can complete a Miracle Morning. During my Miracle Morning, I usually do some yoga stretches to get my body warmed up, but you can use anything that will make your body engage in some activity! Exercise is the chance for you to give your body the physical care it needs. On some days, if time was running short, I would look up a 5-minute workout on YouTube and just do it in my room.

Just like I prepare for the rest of the Miracle Morning ahead of time, I set out my workout clothes the night before. Depending on what my schedule looks like that day, I either go to the gym for a workout class, or do a workout in my room. You would be surprised by how much stronger you can get through short workouts done in your room. I had a goal to hold a 3-minute plank, followed by 30 sit-ups and then 30 pushups. I called it my "3-30-30." I started off very weak and had to take multiple breaks. I even broke up those goals into three sections to spread throughout the day. So in the mornings, I would wake up my core with a 1-miunte plank, then roll over on my mat straight into 10 sit-ups and then right back onto my hands to do 10 pushups. My roommates watched me struggle with every second of the plank, each sit-up, and each pushup. However, I never gave up. Each day, I got 1% stronger. I was happy because I was working on my health goals in small actionable steps.

I strongly believe that even small bursts of exercise are better than doing nothing at all, and you can make it fun! During my senior year, my roommates and I were all science majors and we would all get really stressed during certain times in the semester. During those times, we knew we needed to let go of stress by having a dance party in our apartment. We would play some Beyoncé music and either sing it loud or lip-sync it for dramatic effect. We would jump up and down and dance our stress out. We would all be out of breath by the end of that dance party. It was honestly a good workout! Not only did we take a fun break, but we brought oxygen into our brains and through our bodies, which was going to help us finish our work.

My point is that you can do anything you want to take care of your health, as long as it promotes movement. You can go to a Zumba class, register for an actual dance or yoga class that becomes a part of your school schedule, take a walk, or go for a run listening to your favorite music in the world. You can go golfing, you can climb the stairs in your dorm up and down, or you can even do cartwheels and handstands if you want to! The sillier your exercise is, the better! Whatever you choose to do, make sure it is an activity you *want* to do every day, not something you *have* to do. It is not about becoming thin or super buff; rather, it is about taking care of the body that will carry you forward in your personal and academic journey. You deserve to be happy, strong, and energized. Give yourself that gift.

Another gift you should give yourself is the gift of sleep. Many college students think that it is normal to have many late nights, but it actually impacts their health. By maximizing your time during the day through foundational scheduling, you should be able to limit those late nights drastically. Sleeping will give your body the time it needs to rest. Sleep is beneficial for so many reasons, but I would say the best reason of all is that you will not feel like a zombie the next day. Committing to the Miracle Morning does not mean that you are sleeping less. It just means that you have to be more conscious of how you prioritize your time so you do get enough sleep each night. Your Miracle Morning is customizable to you. I used to do shorter versions of it during the week and longer ones on the weekends. Figure out the Miracle Morning routine that works best for you, and make sure you plan your sleep schedule around that. Sleep is so important for your development during college; make sure you prioritize it.

I also found that visiting a chiropractor was really helpful. Having a healthy spine is a reflection of the quality of the physical health you live out day by day. I remember there were times that my neck and back would hurt from heavy backpacks, or from sitting in a poor posture for hours as I worked on a paper or studied. Chiropractic adjustments were super effective in maintaining my health. I found myself breathing more easily, and feeling aligned helped me work more efficiently. I highly recommend going to a chiropractor for adjustments at least once a month as a way of taking care of your health. I am proud to say that my brother, George Janji, is a future chiropractor, and I am happy to see his passions align with that work. (I can also get free adjustments for the rest of my life, so I'm not complaining!)

Health is a journey for us all, and along my journey I have connected with someone I look up to and respect in the health and fitness industry. Her name is Andrea B. Riggs; I introduced her briefly earlier in the book. Andrea has been in the health and fitness industry for nearly a decade. As I've learned more about her, I have come to understand that health is not just about dieting and calories; it runs deeper than that, and is connected to absolutely every aspect of our lives. Andrea understands this and has created programs such as www.metabod.com (a complete fitness and nutritional program to educate clients about their bodies and nutrition) and www.fermentationforlife.com (centered on healing the gut). While these concepts may seem very unsexy at our age, the truth is that the food we eat, the way we internalize our world, and the way we move our bodies matters. Andrea has held what seems like every fitness certification imaginable and has also been the Motivational Movement Expert at The Miracle Morning conferences called The Best Year Ever (Blueprint) since their inception in 2014. She is truly the best in the business! Make sure to check her out at those two URLs.

MENTAL/EMOTIONAL HEALTH

LMU students are very intelligent and passionate people. They are always involved in many time-consuming commitments. Most are full-time students, have a job, internship, or assistantship, and are members of Greek Life or service organization. They choose to be busy students. On the outside, they tend to seem happy, responsible and organized, and always have continued success. They look like they are able to do it all! I always found myself comparing myself to my peers at LMU, but in reality I was not handling it well. Through my research, I found that I was not alone in my struggles.

One day, I came across a New York Times article, "Suicide and the Pressure of Perfection," from July 2015. The article talked about six University of Pennsylvania students who committed suicide in a 13-month span. The writer described students' mental health by explaining the concept of the Duck Syndrome: "A duck appears to glide calmly across the water, while beneath the surface, it frantically, relentlessly paddles." Students who appeared to have it "all together" actually did not. In an effort to be successful during their time in college, the students kept saying "yes" to every opportunity that came their way, and in turn, kept saying "no" to their own health, dreams, and goals. After further research I came across another alarming statistic. According to Active Minds, Inc., **1,100 college students die by suicide each year** (http://activeminds.org/).

I just could not believe how much we were struggling as young people with our mental health. Although I realized that I was not alone in my struggles, I did not find any comfort in knowing that my peers were probably struggling with their mental health. I wanted to gather some data about the mental health of LMU students. I found that of the one thousand students who used the psychological services on campus during LMU's 2015–2016 school year, the Clinician Index of Concerns (CIC) revealed that 39.2% students came in for depression, and 66.7% came in for anxiety. It is important to note that these are not medical diagnoses, but a reflection of what the student comes in for. Even though that represented only about one-sixth of the LMU student population, I couldn't ignore that a thousand students came in for psychological support. It's impossible to know how many more students having trouble chose not to use the psychological services on campus.

The American College Health Association, the nation's principal advocate and leadership organization for college and university health, delivered a survey called the National College Health Assessment II (ACHA NCHA II) to 93,000 students at 108 different colleges. In the Spring 2015 Reference Group, 30% of students reported that stress had negatively affected their academic performances. In this same study, almost 90% of students reported that they felt constantly overwhelmed. This happens because students are unable to find the balance among their academics, social life, and health; consequently, they are unhappy in their daily lives.

Unfortunately, the statistics do not seem to be improving for students. According to a study done in 2014 by the National Survey of College Counseling Centers that was sponsored by the American College Counseling Association (ACCA), directors of college counseling centers reported that over the previous five years there had been an 89% increase in students with anxiety disorders. In addition, this study also reported that over half of college students feel hopeless and do not know how to get out of their situation. As a result of these mental health issues, students can't perform their best academically.

Hal says something that fits right in with this topic: "Give up being perfect for being authentic." Where did this unattainable standard of perfection come from? You were told you have to do well so you can land a good job, or get into grad school … so you work until you break down. It is true to a certain extent that doing well in college can give you more opportunities, but I dare to ask: *At what cost?*

The statistics do not lie. There is a real problem with students who struggle with mental health. I know this from personal experience.

During the fall semester of my junior year, I was already overwhelmed and stressed out, even though it was only the third week of the semester. With every new semester, I believed that I would be able to handle it all. I was in a major that I was not excelling in. I was unhappy all the time. I used to watch funny YouTube clips all day to help me forget about the problems I had. I would binge-watch shows on Netflix until my brain became numb. I would eat really unhealthy meals and was too depressed to exercise. I would just watch as time passed by too slowly. I did not want to tell my parents how stressed I was so that they would not become worried. I was constantly telling them lies about how I was doing on my exams. My parents and my brother slowly caught on that I was actually not doing well in any area of my life.

On a random day, my dad called me around five in the afternoon and said that he was going to pick me up from school and take me out to dinner. We drove to Manhattan Beach, walked on the pier for a little while, and then went to a nearby restaurant. During dinner, my father looked at me and simply asked, "How are you?" I could not hide it from him anymore, and I started crying right there. I told him the truth about everything that was going on. He told me that I should have quit the extra-curricular activities that were not serving my growth a long time ago, because my health comes first. He convinced me to quit my job the next day in order to salvage the classes I had left. Within 48 hours, I had moved out of my RA room and into another dorm. My mom knew how sad I was, and would drive over to LMU every few weeks to bring me some food from home. I spent the next two months of that semester trying to take care of myself, even though I was still depressed. Ultimately, I failed a few classes that semester.

Please, learn from my mistakes. When you put your health first, everything else in your life thrives, including your academics. Using the time management tips discussed in Chapter 7, discern whether the opportunities coming your way align with your priorities. When it comes to your health, it is okay to say "no" to opportunities that are taking time away from your well-being, academics, and social life. You can actually feel if something is not making you feel happy or grateful. In those moments, it is important to make a bold decision to say "yes" for your peace of mind and "no" to opportunities that may look great at first. **Learning how to say "no" is a skill that they do not teach you in school, so it is important for you to practice it for yourself.** What may be a "yes" to someone else may be a "no" for you. Be in tune with your heart and make the decisions that will bring you closer to gratitude and radiant health.

When it comes to your mental state, seek help early and often. There is not a day that I regret seeing a psychologist. After the crisis in my junior year, I began following the Life S.A.V.E.R.S. and slowly built myself up. *Silence* gave me the clarity I needed to continue improving. *Affirmations* became my cheerleader for success. *Visualization* helped me watch my own movie, and I directed it in every angle I wanted to. *Exercise* gave me an outlet to release my frustrations, while also improving my mental and emotional health. *Reading* gave me insight into myself in ways I never imagined. *Scribing* gave me the space to write out all the thoughts in my head and helped me remain grateful and determined for my future. Each day, I gained awareness of my thoughts and the areas in my life that needed improving. Taking care of myself actually made me a better student. I am happy for the leaps that I took to care for myself, because it rewarded me abundantly.

ENVIRONMENTAL HEALTH

Just like who you surround yourself with affects your state of mind, your physical surroundings have a significant impact on your health. During the stressful phases of a semester, I noticed that my room became really messy, which was not conducive to efficient work. The time I spent looking for things in my room could have been spent studying more or getting work done. Physical clutter actually becomes a form of mental clutter and can block your brain from being in complete focus.

Everything in your immediate reach can either harm or benefit your health. When I realized how my surroundings affected my health, I started to ask myself what was important for me to have in my room, and how I wanted everything organized. I used to have a lot of decorations all over my walls that served as affirmations, but I realized they were playing a bigger role as decorations. I spent a lot more time sitting at my desk than anywhere else, which means I was not staring at my walls for inspiration. I decided to remove anything on my desk that was distracting me. I replaced those items with all my affirmations and pictures from my vision board. Having those words and images right next to my desk helped me focus and get back to my work. (If you do not do your homework in your room, you can put your affirmations and pictures that inspire you to get work done into computer documents, print them, and take them with you wherever you choose to study.) Reminding yourself *why* you are committed to completing your work is very important.

Next, I organized my closet and drawers. Instead of having my jackets, shirts, and pants all mixed with each other in the closet, I separated them so everything would be easier to find. In my drawers, I organized my clothing in a way that I planned all my outfits at the beginning of the week. I would have one drawer for shirts and another for pants, and another for my workout clothes. When I woke up, I chose the first shirt and pants that were on each stack, and did not second-guess it. There is no reason to waste time on choosing your clothes. Automate that system for yourself! I wanted to have all the time I could for my Miracle Morning, and having my clothes for that day already planned at the beginning of the week made it very easy for me to get ready for class.

Pro Tip #1: You would be surprised by how much more clean and organized your room looks just by making your bed every morning. This is how my mornings begin: My phone is usually very far from my bed, so that when my alarm goes off, I have to get out of bed and walk over to turn it off. Instead of getting back into bed, I walk straight to the bathroom, brush my teeth, and drink a tall glass of water. These mindless activities help my brain wake up and increase my wake up motivation level (WUML). Only after I am mildly awake, I walk back in and make my bed. This keeps me from feeling like crawling back into bed, and gets me ready to start my Miracle Morning. After I close my bed, it feels as if everything is in place and my room is already clean to start the day.

Pro Tip #2: Each night before I sleep, I try to put everything back in its place, which never takes more than five minutes. This keeps my room clean throughout the semester, even during times of high stress. There have been times I have had to clean my room for hours because I let the mess add on top of each other. If you break that down into five minutes of cleaning each night and making your bed each morning, you'll be off to a great start.

SPIRITUAL HEALTH

During my time at LMU, I quickly learned the power of spiritual health in my life. Whether you are spiritual, religious, or neither, it is important to find stillness and look inward for reflection. This can be done through meditation, yoga, or attending a religious service. LMU is founded on the Jesuit and Marymount traditions, and there was a chapel on campus. As a student, I found that going to mass, especially the student masses on campus, helped me clear my mind and set my intentions for the week. Journaling is another way you can practice improving your spiritual health, because as you journal more often, you are able to be more connected to yourself and all the experiences around you.

There is something else you must do that will carry you through the hardest times in your life and will help you feel fulfilled by your work. It is the act of *giving*. Since 2014, I have been volunteering at Marycrest Manor, a convalescent home for the elderly. I started going there to complete the service hours required for my service organization on campus. Whenever I go there, I act as my goofy self around the residents in attempts to make them laugh. Knowing that I am able to make someone smile truly makes my day, and the residents always smile and laugh, whether I am singing or dancing to them. As I continued being myself alongside them, I began to feel more whole. It was as if they were giving me meaning, even though I went there to entertain them. I first started volunteering there to fulfill service hours, but now I visit because I need them more than they need me.

No matter how hard we work to succeed personally or academically, we must realize that our work is not solely for us. Our work is for others! Your success gives someone the freedom to believe that they can also achieve at a higher level. We live in an interdependent world. We have a responsibility to help as many people as we can, because it will shape the world we will live in. There is always more that you and I can give, and in that act we receive things that are intangible, like hope, strength, significance, and vitality.

During your time in college, I highly suggest you engage in volunteer work at least once a month. You can donate blood, visit a convalescent home, tutor at a nearby middle school, or volunteer at a domestic violence or homeless shelter. You can go on volunteermatch. org to find a volunteer activity that you like to do. The options are limitless. There are people who need your help, and you will find that the people you serve will give you more than you give to them. Every person in the world deserves love and hope, and you have the power to contribute your light.

When your work has a purpose that is bigger than you, you will overcome every obstacle you are faced with on your journey. It will give you a sense of urgency toward your work, an internal energy that will fuel you beyond what you thought was possible. What you do impacts everyone around you: your friends, family, and even those you do not know yet. Having a heart of service will always inspire you to do more and be more on the path of your dreams.

Lastly, practice gratitude. There is a quote from Melody Beattie that perfectly explains the power of practicing gratitude: *"Gratitude unlocks the fullness of life. It turns what we have into enough, and more. It turns denial into acceptance, chaos to order, and confusion to clarity. It can turn a meal into a feast, a house into a home, a stranger into a friend."* Writing down each day all the things you are grateful for brings you to the present moment, and it makes you appreciate the fullness of your life. Appreciating where you are in your life right now allows you to have the positive energy to improve your life. When you form the habit of writing down what you are grateful for each day, you will realize that there is always more to be grateful than ungrateful for. Gratitude will give you the fuel to continue on your journey.

WHEN YOU'RE IN THOSE MOMENTS

I hope you are able to see now how health is the basis of your success. Your health will give you the energy to accomplish your goals. You can achieve Level 10 health if you follow the advice I've given you above. However, most people do not remember the actions they can take in situations of stress, sadness, depleted energy, anger, frustration, anxiety, or depression. Even I forget to do things that I know could help me! Our mind just shuts off all the ideas that could get us out of our funk and back to a place of gratitude. I needed to find something that would remind me of what usually works for me in certain situations. I wanted to put reminders for myself in all the places I am usually looking. I typed something like this for myself and put copies of it all around my room:

"Actions to take when I am feeling...

- **Overwhelmed:** Deep breaths
- **Frustrated:** Find peace if it is something I cannot change
- **Sluggish:** Make sure I am hydrated, or take a nap
- **Anxious:** Read my affirmations that bring me back to the present moment
- **Exhausted:** Take care of myself; sleep early
- **Depressed:** Write as many things as I can think of that I am grateful for
- **Stressed:** Take deep breaths, review affirmations, visualize getting through the obstacle
- ...."

As I continued growing my awareness of my own mind, I recognized the emotions that I felt most frequently in my life. For example, I realized that when I am feeling overwhelmed, my mind is usually hyperactive, and I feel as though I cannot breathe deeply. One action I take when I am overwhelmed is to take out my laptop and start to free-write what I think and feel about what's going on in my life. What I usually find is that there are a lot of things masking the true source of what is making me feel overwhelmed. When I identify that one thing, I then ask myself the question: "Is there anything I can do to solve this challenge?" If there is, I take action on it. Then, I feel relieved, as if all the other little things melted away, too!

When doing this exercise, write out the emotions that you feel during school. Additionally, think about the ways you cope with your problems. Are those ways constructive, or destructive? Once you have identified a certain emotion, think about what your future self would tell you to do, then write it down next to that emotion. This way, when you are feeling a certain way, you've already thought through what can help you, and you can jump right into improving your health.

Mantras

What I found after doing the previous exercise is that creating short mantras or phrases that I can easily memorize and repeat to myself can really help me in my day-to-day life. A couple of mantras that have helped me in my life are:

Do, Not Worry.

Be Here.

I came up with *"Do, Not Worry"* (yes, the comma is meant to be there) when I recognized that I used to worry about everything in my life, but never took action. When I used to complain to other people, their usual response was "Don't worry, Natalie! It will all work out." In that response, I was told to not worry, but I was not *doing* anything about it. Since then, every time I have found myself getting worried, I repeat the mantra *"Do, Not Worry"* as a reminder to do something about my worries instead of just talking about them.

"Be Here" originated because I found that I was in my head with my thoughts to such a degree that I was not aware of the present

moment. I would replay my *past* over and over in my head and worry about the *future*, even though the past and the future do not exist. The past is gone, and the future has not happened yet! The only thing that does exist is the present moment. *Be Here* reminds me to enjoy and think about only what I have to accomplish today, not about what I didn't accomplish yesterday, or what I need to do tomorrow. Being present is calming, too.

When I was struggling with my mental health, I used to hate that I would get depressed, and how anxious I was all the time. My dad told me something I would never forget: "*Natalie, it is normal to become depressed, anxious, or anything else. What is important is how fast you get out of that state.*" If I could change a few words of that, I would change it to, "*Natalie, it is normal to become depressed, anxious, or anything else. What is important is how fast you* **become aware** *of* **your current** *state.*"

First, awareness will give you the mental clarity to realize where you are now, and will allow you to find what can help you in that moment. Second, the way you are feeling at that moment is not permanent. You will not always be anxious, depressed, or unhappy. It is all *temporary.* Just as you were happy before you became overwhelmed, you can be overwhelmed before you are at peace again. One mantra can be exactly what you need to change it all. You get to choose whether you want to get out of a state of mind that is not serving you to a state of mind that does. Awareness is a muscle you strengthen … you just have to practice!

CONCLUDING THOUGHTS

The best part about taking care of your health is that you always have the power to improve your circumstances. Your existence means that there is always hope. You are capable, worthy, and deserving of Level 10 health. Everybody has something that they want to improve on for their health. The Miracle Morning is here to support you on your journey with health and vitality!

You have read about how to achieve Level 10 College Student Success in the areas of Academics, Social Life, and Health. This triad is the core of your college career. On your Miracle Morning journey as a college student, you will grow into the person ready for life after graduation. Let's get right into Chapter 10!

— 10 —

Exceptional College Student Success Skill #4:

PREP FOR POST-GRADUATION

Why not go out on a limb? That's where the fruit it is.
—MARK TWAIN

Music: "Find My Way"
by THE GABE DIXON BAND

After years of going to classes, taking tests, writing what felt like a million papers and doing all those presentations, you will one day wake up and it will be your graduation day! Your friends and family will be with you cheering you on, chanting your name from their seats as you walk up to the stage to receive your diploma. It is the moment you have been working for years to reach, the one vision that is *finally* coming true!

Your journey started from the very beginning of college. Actually, it started before that. It started in high school when you made the decision to go to college. You filled out all those applications and took those standardized tests. Then in college you worked hard to get good grades. Maybe you did an internship with an incredible organization. You may have joined many clubs or taken on leadership positions. You worked hard on all your final papers, presentations, and exams. Maybe you even presented at a conference, just to get more leverage to have the success you want. You are on the verge of success, so close to reaching the goal of getting your degree.

I graduated from Loyola Marymount University in 2016. A few months after my graduation, some of my friends from the incoming senior class of LMU started reaching out to me. They would start by asking me, "Natalie, what is life like after graduation?" Then, they would follow up that question with, "What do you *do* during the day?"

I remember when I was a senior asking myself those questions, too. I'd think to myself, *Seriously, what do people do after they graduate?* It's like magic. One day, they are on campus, and then Poof! They're gone! What are they so busy doing? I could not imagine what the world outside of LMU was because I was just so used to being in school and doing student-y things. You and I have been in school pretty much our entire lives, so we cannot recognize a life that does not have academic structure, a life without classes, papers, exams, or things to complete for a grade. It is the *certainty* of knowing where you will be at exactly what time on any given day. That's what we got used to!

I started getting a full picture of the fear I had of leaving college as my friends were revealing their fears to me about life after graduation. Their fear was masking the real opportunity here: the opportunity of freedom! I remember telling myself, "Why do I have to leave college?" yet the question I should have asked myself is, "What do I get to do now that I am finished with college?" You finally have the freedom to choose what you want to do on any given day.

If I had a dollar for every time someone asked, "Are you ready for 'the real world'?" I would have paid off my entire student loan before even graduating. The phrase "the real world," or any similar phrase that connotes the difficulty of day-to-day life, has always been something that bothers me, and not many things bother me. Every time I came back from a small trip, my dad would pick me up from the airport and he would say, "I hope you had fun! Now it's *back to reality.*" Back to reality? Isn't this *all* my reality? What was I coming back from, fantasy?

It got me thinking: *How might I go about creating a life that I would be happy to call my reality?*

THE JOURNEY ~~TO "THE REAL WORLD"~~ TO FINDING THE RIGHT QUESTIONS

During my senior year, the thoughts in my head kept circulating as I tried to find an answer to the question: *How might I go about creating a life that I would be happy to call my reality?* I felt the power in that question, and I knew I had to find the answer to it. Little did I know how far asking that question was going to take me!

In the last six months, I have been a participant in co-creating the futures of organizations I care about by using the process of Appreciative Inquiry. In *The Joy of Appreciative Living* by Jacqueline Kelm, Appreciative Inquiry is explained as "A positive, strength-based approach to organizational change distinguished by 'the co-evolutionary search for the best in people, their organizations, and the relevant world around them.'" It is an approach to change organizations by focusing on what is working in an organization, rather than what is not working.

When was the last time we thought about what is going *right* in our lives? During my senior year, I used to think about all the things I did not do to prepare myself for success after graduating. I thought about all the C's on my transcript, the depression and anxiety I had throughout college, and the classes I failed and had to retake.

Thinking about all these things made me feel disempowered. I made me feel as though I did not have many options to succeed in my future. Yet when I asked, *How might I go about creating a life that I would be happy to call my reality?* I realized that my life is in my hands today, not in the past.

David Cooperrider conceptualized Appreciative Inquiry in 1980 as his doctoral thesis at Case Western Reserve University with his thesis advisor Suresh Srivastava. It is still being used today by The Flourishing Leadership Institute to facilitate strengths-based, rapid, whole-system change to organizations and communities. Cooperrider used Appreciative Inquiry with the Cleveland Clinic in 1985, where he made many discoveries. His first discovery was this: *The questions we ask are fateful. Questions change the lens through which we see the world.* When you put on your glasses or your contact lenses, you do not necessarily look at the lens, you look *through* the lens. Through this discovery, we find that the questions we ask ourselves are the lenses through which we see the world. So when students ask themselves *Why am I not smart enough?* or *How am I ever going to get through school?* they are belittling their intelligence and creating resistance to the idea of being able to graduate college, respectively.

When I asked the question, *How might I go about creating a life that I would be happy to call my reality?* I was valuing the best of who I was, what I might become, how I might design my life with my strengths, and how to deploy that plan. Appreciative Inquiry allows you to work toward the future with higher aspirations by focusing on the positive emotions.

Asking the right questions continued to play a defining role in creating the life I wanted after graduation. I asked myself the question: *What pursuits make me excited for my future?* This question allowed my mind to want to choose a future filled with adventure. In the opaque visions I saw of myself, I came up with a few ideas that made me excited about my future:

- **I wanted to study French.** After studying abroad in Germany, I realized how much I loved learning languages. Learning a language is not only productive and good for your mental health, it is also a lot of fun! I decided to sign up for a French class at a nearby community college.

- **I wanted to learn how to cook, and to spend more time with my family.** Both of my grandmas are amazing cooks, and they had so many Armenian traditions and recipes to pass down to me. I wanted to use this time I had to spend more time with my grandmas for some lessons. Additionally, I wanted to spend time with my younger cousins who were growing up so quickly!

- **I wanted to take care of my health.** I really wanted to become stronger and faster, and I was able to dedicate of lot of time to achieving that after I graduated.

- **I wanted to write a book.** I had many ideas in mind, but one idea kept screaming louder than all the rest. I wanted to write a book for college students.

I felt very strongly about doing things I was passionate for, and these ideas made me really excited. I was not going to back down. I wanted to prove that it was okay to do something I wanted after college, even if it did not feel safe.

I kept thinking about a book for college students, and it felt *good.* It felt right. I had ideas running around in my mind already, and I felt like I had so much to write. I found myself giving advice to younger students all the time. I wanted them to feel that they were not alone in their struggles, even if it might seem that way. I wanted to write a book that had everything students would need to succeed. In writing out all my ideas, I realized that I would not have improved as an individual or as a student if not for *The Miracle Morning* book I read my junior year. So I took a leap! I decided that I was going to create *The Miracle Morning for College Students*, even if Hal did not know it yet.

For the next week, I spent every living and free moment to ask myself the right questions to (1) convince Hal that I should be the coauthor, and (2) gain the right direction to write the book that college students need. I sat for hours writing down all the questions

I needed to answer to make this proposal the best proposal he would receive. A list of 30 questions jumpstarted me on the project and got me writing. After many painful edits and writing in the odd hours past midnight, I had a comprehensive proposal that concisely and beautifully stated everything that Hal needed to know.

I sent it to him and waited for a response. I was waiting for some kind of confirmation email that he had received my proposal, but I had to ask for it, because I was thoroughly worried that my email got caught in a spam filter or something. Two weeks later, I got an email confirming that they had received my email, thanking me for wanting to help students, and saying that they would contact me once they had reviewed the proposal. It was exciting for me to hear that, yet so nerve-racking, too. I had to keep it a secret from my parents, because I did not want to get their hopes up in case it did not go further than that email. It was something too big to share in the beginning.

I visited San Diego for my brother's birthday. It had been three months of silence by then. I had a few hours to type out a message that asked for some kind of response about the proposal I had sent Hal. I had seen that Hal was going to hold a live event in Chicago in just a few weeks, and I was so sure that if I saw him face-to-face, I could convince him to give me this opportunity to coauthor the book. I just needed a chance.

The following day at 6:45 a.m., during my Miracle Morning, I sent Hal a long email, probably too long. You know how people tell you that you should not send important people very long emails because it is a waste of their time? Well, I sent it anyways, and then entered my 7 a.m. gym class. I just let it go, and during that one hour, I tried to remain focused on my health instead of worrying about whether I would get a response. When the class was over, I grabbed my bag and checked my phone. By the time I had reached my car, I saw that I had an email from Hal. After three months of silence, I got an email response from him in one hour.

Without hesitation, I called my parents and told them over the phone the secret that I had kept from them for three months, and that I was about to buy my ticket to Chicago for Hal's event happening in

10 days. During that drive home, I was crying, because for the first time in three months, I knew that I was going to do it. I was going to make Hal and his team believe that I should be the coauthor. I went home, and in the next hour I bought my ticket to the event and my flight to Chicago.

With this opportunity of seeing Hal and his team, I did not want to leave anything to chance. I knew that I had to do everything in my power to be ready when I met Hal and Honorée. I asked myself, how could I be prepared at a moment's notice to sell the idea of *The Miracle Morning for College Students* and get chosen as the coauthor? In those 10 days, I prepared an hour-long presentation, typed up a single-page handout to give to every attendee of that live event, and got my book proposal ready. I went to Kinko's the midnight before my trip and printed out 10 copies of my PowerPoint slides, 215 copies of my handout, and 20 copies of the proposal that I had written months before. I put that Kinko's box in my carryon because I wanted it next to me at all times.

During my first day in Chicago, I asked about the possibility of adding this title to *The Miracle Morning* book series. I was told that I would have to wait two years to add this book to the series, without the promise that I would be the coauthor. Discouraged, I went back to my hotel room that night, grateful that my brother came on the trip with me for moral support. When I arrived at the room, I told him that I would have to wait two years without the guarantee that I would be the author. My brother turned to me and asked, "How badly do you want it?!"

I had a decision to make. I could walk away and work on something else instead of potentially wasting two years waiting for this opportunity, or I could work on improving myself and my writing skills for two years and become the person worthy of being the coauthor. In the end, I could not shake off this dream. *I just wanted it so badly!* I couldn't sweep it under the rug. My brother looked at me and said, "We are going to do this together." I called my parents and told them my decision, and they told me they would help me in any way they could. I slept that night grateful for the support I had around me, and feeling that fire inside me that would not die with any obstacle that would come my way.

Your life can change at any one moment. You know the ending to this story. :)

I wanted to share the nuggets of knowledge I found within my journey as it will apply to the rest of your life!

There is no "right path" after graduating.

Lots of students think about what they *should* be doing as opposed to all they *can* do. When I entered my senior year as a chemistry major, I looked into graduate schools, chemist jobs, environmental chemistry lab tech positions, the whole nine yards. I kept asking myself: *What should I do with this major?* Some people will choose to go to graduate school, some will choose to enter the workforce, some will choose post-graduate service, some will travel, and some will do nothing. There is no "right path" because the path is your life. It is up to you what you want to do with it. The best part is, you can do and be anything. If I did not expand my vision beyond my major, this book would not exist. Ask the right questions to design the path you want to live.

Opportunities do not show up at your front door. You have to create them for yourself.

I wanted to do *big* things with my life, and I was not going to let my current circumstance of mediocre grades dictate my future. Just because I did not want to go to graduate school or explore the other post-graduate options around me did not mean that I was going to be a failure. If I wanted something in my life, I was going to work for it and create it myself. I was going to deliberately design my life with the Miracle Morning and make sure that I lived the life that most spoke to the center of my existence, a life that I was proud to live.

There are opportunities out there waiting to be seized! Your college or university has connections with many companies and organizations that have jobs waiting for someone like you. Your professors know many people in their field that they can connect you to, which can be the bridge to a great internship that will lead to a job you love. The most important part is that you make the effort to enlist those you have developed relationships with during your time in school to help you find those opportunities you seek. Do not wait for an opportunity to show up at your door. The brain you have is capable of amazing things, and one of those things is creating opportunities in your life!

If your dreams don't scare you, they aren't big enough.

In the book *Visions to the Top*, hall of fame salesperson and successful entrepreneur Justin Ledford writes, "People sometimes get so caught up with work, TV shows, and daily habits that they forget to dream." When was the last time you dreamed? When was the last time you had a dream that was so big it scared you? Stop reading for just a few minutes, and dream. Open your mind and your heart to whatever you've been blocking out for too long.

We all have dreams. Tap into yours, and feel alive again! You will feel inspired within yourself, like you are being pulled to a greater existence. You will feel your heart start to race, your mind start to create visuals of what you want to happen, and a buzzing energy start to flow throughout your body. Feel that fire inside your heart again, the one you have dimmed for far too long. Grab it! Keep it! Do not let it go! Journal it, write it down. If you do not pursue it, you will always live with regret for never trying. You have the potential to make a difference for someone, or in the world, more than you think. What have you got to lose? You have everything to gain. If you can dream it, it is possible.

You have to believe in yourself and your ideas more than any-one else ever can or will. If you don't, people will try to steer you away from your dreams.

Find the reasons within yourself that will keep you on your path. Many people will try to steer you away from those dreams because they want you to live the dream they have for you. They will tell you that their dream for you is more important than your dream for yourself. They will not even recognize what they are doing! You have to believe in yourself and your ideas forever, and you will gather the people who also believe in your dreams along the way. Be like a tree: You may be swayed by the wind but you remain rooted in your truth. (You can thank my Mom for the tree metaphors.)

As much as I met with support for my dream of writing this book, I was also met with resistance from many. You may be surprised by the people who don't support you even when you believe you are doing something amazing and good for others. As long as you know the good you are doing for others, then the naysayers do not matter.

Many people are afraid to pursue their own dreams and fail, and that is why they fear when others pursue their dreams. Their resistance to your dreams stems from their own fears. By working hard for your dreams, you allow those people to realize that they can also go after their dream. There is nothing more beautiful than giving someone that freedom. I have seen it happen with the people around me.

Additionally, for the sake of your friends and family, do not limit your own dreams. By limiting your dreaming, you constrict someone in their ability to live theirs. You only have one shot at life: Make it a good one. Dream big, and then dream bigger than that! Rise up, and bring everyone with you along for the ride.

Surround yourself with people who believe in you and support you, and be that support for them as well.

As I wrote about earlier in the book, the people you surround yourself with are extremely important for your success. Those who will support you through all your moments, the good and the bad, are the ones to keep close. Be there for them, too. Your circle of influence, your front row, is not a one-way relationship. You need to be there for them just as they are there for you. Be in the front row for them, and cheer them on. You will not be able to succeed if you do not want others to succeed. Pick them up when they are down.

There will always be obstacles on your path. How you respond to them will be your greatest asset.

Have you ever accomplished something fulfilling and significant that did not have obstacles? Of course not! Life's most exciting moments are when we overcome obstacles and achieve our goals. Everything worth accomplishing comes with obstacles. The roadblocks will come, but that is a good thing. It means that you are on the right path. The path of least resistance will get you nowhere.

Hard work pays off. Having unwavering faith pays off. Every obstacle that comes your way is the universe's way of giving you a choice: to run away from your dreams, or to keep moving forward. Every successful person in history overcame many obstacles. They say it takes more than ten years to become an overnight success. Wake up each morning with the Miracle Morning and visualize going through each obstacle with determination. You will gain knowledge from them to take with you throughout your journey. Be grateful for your obstacles and use them as stepping stones to get closer to your accomplishments.

Have a Why that is bigger than you.

When you have a *why* that is rooted in serving others, you will feel pulled to work more until your task is done. There will be many difficult days where you will want to give up. I've even experienced my own difficulty while writing this book. Having a big *why* has always given me perspective and reminded me how important it is to get my work done. I am passionate about helping college students, and that is why I strive. Imagine having a *why* so big that you spring out of bed because you cannot wait to help others. Your Miracle Morning routine is going to get you there.

WHAT IS YOUR LEVEL 10 JOURNEY?

As graduation was approaching, I felt nervous, but I was committed to living a Level 10 post-graduate life. I am grateful to be living my Level 10 life, but I made sure I was creating my path by asking the right questions. Now it is your turn. Let's dream for a few minutes:

- What does a Level 10 post-graduation life look like to you?
- What are your biggest hopes and dreams?
- What is your life's passion?
- What do you love to do?
- What are you best at?
- What problem can you solve?
- How can you add value to the world?
- What dream job do you want to have?
- What kind of environment are you in?
- What kind of people are you around?
- What can you feel, see, hear, smell, and touch?
- Does this vision make you excited? Where do you feel the excitement?

Take a moment to journal and answer these questions. I believe you have all the answers in you. Uncover all your biggest dreams. It is scary to pull them out from under the rug. Give yourself the opportunity to feel alive, to live your one life, to have it your way. Break free from your own chains. Write it all out. The moment you write it, you make it concrete.

In fact, you can even make a vision board! There are so many ways to create one. You can do it the old-fashioned way, by cutting out pictures from magazines or finding them on the Internet, then gluing them all together on a piece of cardboard or heavy paper. You can even print a collage of pictures and make that your vision board. I recently discovered *The Miracle Morning Art of Affirmations: A Positive Coloring Book for Adults and Kids.* It's not only the most positive coloring book out there, but it is a coloring vision board. There is a page where you get to write out and color your vision. Whatever you choose to do, it will not just be some idea that keeps floating around in your brain anymore. You have written it down. There is a reason why you want certain things to happen in your life. Take a leap of faith. Your life and your dreams are always worth it.

Now that you have written it all out, you might be feeling a sense of urgency about what you can do. In the next 10 minutes, what can you do to be one step closer to having your Level 10 post-graduate life? Email someone? Look for that dream job? Follow that dream. Want to apply for Teach for America? Do it! Want to go to graduate school? Do it! You want to go into the Peace Corps? Do it! You want to form a band and go international? Do it! You want to be a mechanic? DO it! Make your life an adventure.

During this time in your life, it is important for you to have the information that will help you get to your vision. *Success for Scholars,* founded by Julian Bradley, is a course that bridges the gap between education and personal development. While you are envisioning your Level 10 journey, the course will be a great resource to help you create a step-by-step plan to start going after the goals that you want to achieve. There is a lot of great knowledge in the course that can help you define your Level 10 journey, too. I highly recommend that you check it out at successforscholars.com.

FIND YOUR PEOPLE

During college, I became involved with a lot of activities on campus, which allowed me to meet many LMU students and faculty. They became the community I loved and cherished at LMU. When you graduate, many of your close friends will not be around you anymore because they will be off living their dreams just as you are living yours. Their dreams may take them back home, to a different state, or to a different country. Everyone has their own path.

When I graduated, I found myself searching for a community that aligned with my values of positivity, self-improvement, and dreaming big. I needed people around me to encourage me in pursuit of my dreams. I began to get more involved with The Miracle Morning

Community online, and also by attending the event in Chicago. The people I met at that event are still people I keep in touch with, because I can say without a doubt that everyone in The Miracle Morning Community is kind, hard-working, and motivated. They work to be the best versions of themselves and want to help others on their journey. Becoming more involved with this community and connecting with many people at the Chicago event has brought me great joy in the months since graduation.

At the Chicago event, I met Tim Rhode, who is the founder of 1Life Fully Lived, a non-profit organization dedicated to mentoring others to dream, plan, and live the life they truly want to live. In the months that I have gotten to know Tim, I can describe him as a dreamer who is your biggest cheerleader. He created this organization to help people live their one life fully, hence its name. His passion to help others has no bounds, and he is a true inspiration. In Chicago, he told me about his event, the 1Life Fully Lived West Coast Conference, which was going to be held in Sacramento a few months later. He urged me to attend and just kept saying, "You don't want to miss it!"

I decided to attend the conference, and I am SO glad I did not miss it. I met many amazing people who are living testaments that anyone can dream, plan, and live their best life. I have met the most kind and passionate individuals, and I am grateful to call them all my friends!

At this event, I found out about the *My 1Life Roadmap*, a course that gives you the life strategies and skills to live the life you want. It will give you the tools to create the life you want in college and beyond. It helps you step by step to develop you from where you are now to where you want to be. In the roadmap, you will be given modules to help you figure out how to plan your journey, understand your finances, and develop the mindset you need so you can live your dreams. I believe it is the course every student needs to take during college!

I am currently taking the course while writing this book, and it has helped me clarify the visions I have for my own life and where I see myself in the next five, ten, and twenty years. It is essential that college students and college graduates take this course. You can take the course in a live version, where you meet up on a video call with the other *My 1Life Roadmap* students to discuss the information learned in that week's module. There is also a DIY version, where you can get the modules and learn the information at your own pace. I am doing the live version of the course. The *My 1Life Roadmap* is one of the *best* steps you can take to invest in yourself at any point in your life. You can email them about student pricing for the roadmap course at my1liferoadmap@1lifefullylived.org, and you should definitely join the 1Life Community on Facebook at facebook.com/groups/1lifefullylived.

Whether you are working toward becoming an accountant, an actor, a teacher, a doctor, a chemist, a writer, or a cinematographer, the Miracle Morning Community, the Miracle Morning for College Students Community, and the 1Life Community are three groups that you should join. Becoming a part of these communities will give you the energy, resources, love, support, and guidance you need to accomplish your dreams. In Chapter 8, we discussed Jim Rohn's quote, "You are the average of the five people you spend the most time with." Getting to know the people in these communities by talking to them, creating accountability, and masterminding with them has the potential to help you evolve into the person you want to become.

IMPROVISE

As you might know, things do not always go as planned in life. You may want one thing to happen, while the universe throws you a curveball—but life is all about improvising. Improvisation is not just a type of acting; it is a way of life.

The moment you get to improvise is the moment directly after something does not go your way. Maybe your alarm clock doesn't go off for your Miracle Morning so you have to do your Life S.A.V.E.R.S. spread throughout the day, or your car breaks down and you have to find another way to work. You might wake up with a sore throat and not want to get out of bed. Your flight might get delayed, or you might find out that you didn't get accepted into graduate school.

These things happen. There are curveballs all the time, and everyone experiences their own adversity. The good news is that we get to make up a reason for why something happened the way it did, and use that to empower us. Whatever life throws at you, you should know that you are only as powerful as your next step. It is what you do in these moments that will determine who you will become. You do not need to know the next ten steps to take, just the next one.

Although these moments may be ones filled with the most confusion, all you need is the Life S.A.V.E.R.S. to help you improvise your new path. You get to use your Miracle Morning to create the space you need to ask yourself the right questions to guide you to your next step. *Silence* will help you find stillness and clarity; *Affirmations* will help you create the confidence you need to improvise your new path; *Visualization* will help you design the imagery of taking your next step with confidence; *Exercise* will give you the mental and physical stamina to continue working toward your dreams; *Reading* will provide you with the knowledge to piece together your improvised vision; *Scribing* will give you the space to assess your thoughts and track your progress along your journey. Lean on the Life S.A.V.E.R.S. through the highs and the lows, and you will find yourself always progressing toward a better you.

The Miracle Morning is a staple in your life now. It is the one thing that will always be there for you. Even if you only have six minutes, you are able to complete a morning routine that will help you become the person you need to be to create your Level 10 life. There are times that something will happen and you might stop doing your morning routine. You will find yourself in an imbalance after that. Don't be so hard on yourself, though. We each have our own areas that need growth. Falling off the routine is not a "failure," but rather a lesson to learn from. Gently guide your way back to the Miracle Morning. The Miracle Morning is not something you *have* to do, but something you *get* to do as a gift to yourself. Whatever obstacle is thrown your way, keep your Miracle Morning as a constant in your life, and you will find yourself grateful and in alignment with your Level 10 vision.

BE BOLD

I believe that living your Level 10 life is a bold opportunity. When I graduated, I had no idea what my future held for me. Instead of facing graduation with fear, I asked myself, *What isn't the future going to hold for me?!* It will be everything I want it to be! You deserve to live the life you desire, and it is completely possible. If you can dream it, then you can do it. You just have to ask for it. Demand it. Don't be afraid to be bold; your dreams are calling for it.

Be Bold.

Be YOU!

— 11 —

THE 30-DAY MIRACLE MORNING CHALLENGE

*An extraordinary life is all about daily, continuous improvements
in the areas that matter most.*

—ROBIN SHARMA

Let's play devil's advocate for a moment. Can the Miracle Morning really transform any area of your life or academics in just 30 days? Can anything really make that significant of an impact, that quickly? Well, remember that it has already done this for thousands of others, and if it works for them, it can and will absolutely work for you.

Incorporating or changing any habit requires an acclimation period, so don't expect this to be effortless from day one. However, by making a commitment to yourself to stick with this, beginning each day with a Miracle Morning and leveraging the Life S.A.V.E.R.S. will quickly become the foundational habit that makes all others possible. Remember: *Win the morning, and you set yourself up to win the day.*

The seemingly unbearable first few days to change a habit are only temporary. While plenty will debate how long it takes to implement a new habit, there is a powerful three-phase strategy that has proven successful for the tens of thousands of individuals who have learned to conquer the snooze button and who now wake up every day for their Miracle Morning.

FROM UNBEARABLE TO UNSTOPPABLE:

The Three-Phase Strategy to Implement Any Habit in 30 Days

As you take the 30-Day Miracle Morning Challenge, here's arguably the simplest and most effective strategy for implementing and sustaining any new habit in just 30 days. This will give you the mindset and approach to adopt as you build your new routine.

Phase One: Unbearable (Days 1–10)

Phase One is when any new activity requires the largest amount of conscious effort, and getting up earlier than you have done before is no different. You're fighting existing habits, the very habits that have been entrenched in *who you are* for years.

In this phase, it's mind over matter—and if you don't mind, it'll definitely matter! Hitting the snooze button and not making the most of your day are habits that hold you back from becoming the superstar college student you have always known you can be. So dig in and hold strong.

In Phase One, while you battle existing patterns and limiting beliefs, you'll find out what you're made of and what you're capable of. You need to keep pushing, stay committed to your vision, and hang in there. Trust me when I say you can do this!

I know it can be daunting on day five to realize you still have 25 days to go before your transformation is complete and you've become a bona fide morning person. Keep in mind that on day five, you're actually more than halfway through the first phase and well on your way. Remember that your initial feelings are not going to last forever. In fact, you owe it to yourself to persevere because, in no time at all, you'll be getting the exact results you want as you become the person you've always wanted to be!

Phase Two: Uncomfortable (Days 11–20)

In Phase Two, your body and mind begin to acclimate to waking up earlier. You'll notice that getting up starts to get easier, but it's not yet a habit—it's not quite who you are and likely doesn't feel natural.

The biggest temptation at this level is to reward yourself by taking a break, especially on the weekends. A question posted quite often in the Miracle Morning Community is, "How many days a week do you get up early for your Miracle Morning?" Our answer—and the one that's most common from longtime Miracle Morning practitioners— is *every single day*.

Once you've made it through Phase One, you're past the hardest period. So keep going! Why on earth would you want to go through that first phase again by taking one or two days off? Trust me, you wouldn't, so don't!

Phase Three: Unstoppable (Days 21–30)

Early rising is now not only a habit, but it has literally become part of *who you are*, part of your identity. Your body and mind will have become accustomed to your new way of being. These next ten days are important for cementing the habit in yourself and your life.

As you engage in the Miracle Morning practice, you will also develop an appreciation for the three distinct phases of habit change. A side benefit is you will realize you can identify, develop, and adopt any habit that serves you—including the habits of exceptional college students that we have included in this book.

Now that you've learned the simplest and most effective strategy for successfully implementing and sustaining any new habit in 30 days, you know the mindset and approach that you need to complete the 30-Day Miracle Morning Challenge. All that's required is for you to commit to get started and follow through.

Consider the Rewards

When you commit to the 30-Day Miracle Morning Challenge, you will be building a foundation for success in every area of your life for the rest of your life. By waking up each morning and practicing the Miracle Morning, you will begin each day with extraordinary levels of *discipline* (the crucial ability to get yourself to follow through with your commitments), *clarity* (the power you'll generate from focusing on what's most important), and *personal development* (perhaps the single most significant determining factor in your success). Thus, in the next 30 days, you'll find yourself quickly becoming the person you need to be to create the extraordinary levels of personal, academic, professional, and future financial success you truly desire.

You'll also be transforming the Miracle Morning from a concept that you may be excited (and possibly a little nervous) to try into a lifelong habit, one that will continue to develop you into the person you need to be to create the life you've always wanted. You'll begin to fulfill your potential and see results in your life far beyond what you've ever experienced before.

In addition to developing successful habits, you'll also be developing the *mindset* you need to improve your life—both internally and externally. By practicing the Life S.A.V.E.R.S. each day, you'll be experiencing the physical, intellectual, emotional, and spiritual benefits of **S**ilence, **A**ffirmations, **V**isualization, **E**xercise, **R**eading, and **S**cribing. You'll immediately feel less stressed, more centered, focused, happier, and more excited about your life. You'll generate more energy, clarity, and motivation to move toward your highest goals and dreams (especially those you've been putting off for far too long).

Remember, your life situation will improve after—but only *after*—you develop yourself into the person you need to be to improve it. That's exactly what these next 30 days of your life can be—a new beginning, and a new you.

You Can Do This!

If you're feeling nervous, hesitant, or concerned about whether you will be able to follow through with this for 30 days, relax—it's completely normal to feel that way. This is especially true if waking up in the morning is something you've found challenging in the past. It's not only expected that you would be a bit hesitant or nervous, but it's actually a very good sign! It's a sign that you're *ready* to commit, otherwise you wouldn't be nervous.

Here we go ...

Taking Action: The 30-Day Miracle Morning Challenge

Now it is time to join the tens of thousands of people who have transformed their lives with *The Miracle Morning*. Join the community online at TMMBook.com and download the toolkit to get you started *today*.

Step 1: Get the 30-Day Miracle Morning Challenge Fast Start Kit

Visit www.TMMBook.com to download your free 30-Day Miracle Morning Challenge Fast Start Kit—complete with the exercises, affirmations, daily checklists, tracking sheets, and everything else you need to make starting and completing the 30-Day Miracle Morning Challenge as easy as possible. Please take a minute to do this now.

Step 2: Plan Your First Miracle Morning for Tomorrow

If you haven't already begun, commit to and schedule your first Miracle Morning as soon as possible—ideally *tomorrow*. Yes, actually write it in your schedule and decide where you will do it. Remember it's recommended that you leave your bedroom to remove yourself from the temptations of your bed altogether. My Miracle Morning takes place every day on my living room couch while everyone else in my house is still sound asleep. I've heard from people who do their Miracle Morning sitting outside in nature, on their porch or deck, or at a nearby park. Do yours where you feel most comfortable, but also where you won't be interrupted.

Step 3: Read Page 1 of the Fast Start Kit and Do the Exercises

Read the introduction in your 30-Day Miracle Morning Challenge Fast Start Kit, then follow the instructions and complete the exercises. Like anything in life that's worthwhile, successfully completing the 30-Day Miracle Morning Challenge requires a bit of preparation. It's important that you do the initial exercises in your Fast Start Kit (which shouldn't take you more than 30–60 minutes), and keep in mind that your Miracle Morning will always start with the *preparation* you do the day or night before to get yourself ready mentally, emotionally, and logistically for the Miracle Morning. This preparation includes following the steps in the Five-Step Snooze-Proof Wake-Up Strategy in chapter 2.

Step 3.1: Get an Accountability Partner (Recommended)

The overwhelming evidence for the correlation between success and accountability is undeniable. While most people resist being held accountable, having someone who will hold us to higher standards than we'll hold ourselves to makes a huge impact on our ability to do what we set out to do. All of us can benefit from the support of an accountability partner, so it's highly recommended—but definitely not required—that you reach out to someone in your circle of influence (family, friend, colleague, significant other, etc.) and enlist their support for the 30-Day Miracle Morning Challenge.

Not only does having someone to hold us accountable increase the odds we will follow through, but joining forces with someone else is simply more fun! Consider that when you're excited about something and committed to doing it on your own, there is a certain level of power in that excitement and your individual commitment. However, when you have someone else who is as excited about it and committed to it as you are, it's much more powerful.

Call, text, or email someone (or more than one!) today, and invite them to join you for the 30-Day Miracle Morning Challenge. The quickest way to get them up to speed is to send them the link to www.MiracleMorning.com so they can get free and immediate access to the Miracle Morning Fast Start Kit, which contains the following:

- The FREE Miracle Morning Video training
- The FREE Miracle Morning Audio training
- Two FREE Chapters of *The Miracle Morning* book

It will cost them nothing, and you'll be teaming up with someone who is also committed to taking their life to the next level, so the two of you can support and encourage each other as well as hold yourselves accountable.

IMPORTANT: Don't wait until you have an accountability partner on board to do your first Miracle Morning and start the 30-Day Miracle Morning Challenge. Whether you've found someone to embark on the journey with you or not, I still recommend scheduling and doing your first Miracle Morning tomorrow—no matter what. Don't wait. You'll be even more capable of inspiring someone else to do the Miracle Morning with you if you've already experienced a few days of it. Get started. Then, as soon as you can, invite a friend, family member, or coworker to visit www.MiracleMorning.com to get their free Miracle Morning Fast Start Kit.

In less than an hour, they'll be fully capable of being your Miracle Morning accountability partner—and probably a little inspired.

Are You Ready to Take Your Life to the Next Level?

What is the next level in your personal or professional life? Which areas need to be transformed for you to reach that level? Give yourself the gift of investing only 30 days to make significant improvements in your life, one day at a time. No matter what your past has been, you *can* change your future by changing the present.

THE MIRACLE EQUATION

by Hal Elrod

There are only two ways to live your life.
One is as though nothing is a miracle.
The other is as though everything is a miracle.

—ALBERT EINSTEIN

You understand now that you *can* wake up early, maintain extraordinary levels of energy, direct your focus, and master the not-so-obvious college student success skills from Natalie. If you also apply what follows to your academics, you're going to go much further: You're going to make your college experience and your life after college truly exceptional.

To make this leap, there is one more helpful tool for you to add to your college student toolbox, and it's called the Miracle Equation.

The Miracle Equation is the underlying strategy that I used to realize my full potential as a salesperson. It has everything to do with how you handle your goals. One of my mentors, Dan Casetta, told me, "The purpose of a goal isn't to hit the goal. The real purpose is to develop yourself into the type of person who can achieve your goals, regardless of whether you hit that particular one or not. It is who you become by giving it everything you have until the last moment— regardless of your results—that matters most."

When you make the decision to stick with a seemingly unachievable goal, despite the fact that the possibility of failure is high, you will become especially focused, faithful, and intentional. When your objective is truly ambitious, it will actually require you to find out what you are really made of!

TWO DECISIONS

As with any great challenge, you need to make decisions related to achieving the goal. You can set a deadline and then create your agenda by asking yourself, *If I were to achieve my goal on the deadline, what decisions would I have to make and commit to in advance?*

And you'll find that, whatever the goal, the two decisions that would make the biggest impact are *always the same.* They form the basis for the Miracle Equation.

THE FIRST DECISION: UNWAVERING FAITH

There was a time in my life when I was trying to achieve an impossible sales goal. I'll use that as an example to show you what I mean. Though this comes from my sales experience, I'll show you how it applies within the context of college (or any situation, really). It was a stressful time, and I was already facing fear and self-doubt, but my thought process about the goal forced me to an important realization. To achieve the seemingly impossible, I would have to maintain unwavering faith every day, *regardless of my results.*

I knew that there would be moments when I would doubt myself and times when I would be so far off track that the goal would no longer seem achievable. But it would be during those moments that I would have to override self-doubt with unshakable faith.

To keep that level of faith in those challenging moments, I repeated what I call my Miracle Mantra:

I will _____ (reach my goal), no matter what. There is no other option.

Understand that maintaining unwavering faith isn't *normal*. It's not what most people do. When it doesn't look like the desired result is likely, average performers give up the faith that it's possible. When the game is on the line, the team is down on the scorecards, and only seconds remain, it is only the top performers—the Michael Jordans of the world—who, without hesitation, tell their team, "Give me the ball."

The rest of the team breathes a sigh of relief because of their fear of missing the game-winning shot. Michael Jordan made a decision at some point in his life that he would maintain unwavering faith, despite the fact that he might miss. (And although Michael Jordan missed 26 game-winning shots in his career, his faith that he would make every single one never wavered.)

That's the first decision that very successful people make, and it's yours for the making, too.

When you're working toward a goal and you're not on track, what is the first thing that goes out the window? *The faith that the outcome you want is possible.* Your self-talk turns negative: *I'm not on track. It doesn't look like I'm going to reach my goal.* And with each passing moment, your faith decreases.

You don't have to settle for that. You have the ability and the choice to maintain that same unwavering faith, no matter what and regardless of the results. This is key in college, because results are often out of your direct control. You may doubt yourself or have a bad day. In the darkest moments, you may wonder if everything will turn out okay. But you must find—over and over again—your faith that all things are possible and hold it throughout your journey, whether it is a 30-day academic goal or a 30-year career.

It's very important that you see your role as a student as directly related to the role of other high-achieving people, because the parallels are unmistakable. If you don't take time to see the parallels here, you may find that you focus on the failures of your academics instead of the successes. And if you focus on the failures, it's hard to reach the goal you want. So stay with me.

Elite athletes maintain unwavering faith that they can make every shot they take. That faith—and the faith you need to develop—isn't based on probability. It comes from a whole different place. Most salespeople operate based on what is known as the *law of averages*. But what we're talking about here is the *law of miracles*. When you miss shot after shot, you have to tell yourself what Michael Jordan tells himself, *I've missed three, but I want the ball next, and I'm going to make that next shot.*

And if you miss that one, *your faith doesn't waiver.* You repeat the Miracle Mantra to yourself:

I will _____ (reach my goal), no matter what. There is no other option.

Then, you simply uphold your integrity and do what it is you say you are going to do.

An elite athlete may be having the worst game ever, where it seems that, in the first three quarters of the game, he can't make a shot to save his life. Yet in the fourth quarter, right when the team needs him, he starts making those shots. He always wants the ball; he always holds belief and faith in himself. In the fourth quarter, he makes three times as many shots as he made in the first three quarters of the game.

Why? Top-performing athletes have conditioned themselves to have unwavering faith in their talents, skills, and abilities regardless of what it says on the scoreboard or their stat sheet.

And …

They combine their unwavering faith with part two of the Miracle Equation: extraordinary effort.

THE SECOND DECISION: EXTRAORDINARY EFFORT

When you allow your faith to go out the window, effort almost always follows right behind it. *After all,* you tell yourself, *what's the point in even trying to achieve your goal if it's not possible?* Suddenly, you wonder how you're ever going to do well academically, let alone reach the big goal you've been working toward.

I've been there many times, feeling deflated and thinking, *What's the point of even trying?* And you might easily think, *There's no way I can make it. I'm too far behind.*

That's where extraordinary effort comes into play. You need to stay focused on your original goal—you need to connect with the vision you had for it, that big *why* in your heart and mind when you set the goal in the first place.

Like me, you need to reverse-engineer the goal. Ask yourself, *If I'm at the end of this month and this goal were to have happened, what would I have done? What would I have needed to do?*

Whatever the answer, you will need to stay consistent and persevere, regardless of your results. You have to believe you can still ring the bell of success at the end. You have to maintain unwavering faith and extraordinary effort—until the buzzer sounds. That's the only way that you create an opportunity for the miracle to happen.

As a college student, your extraordinary effort is to continuously work hard and keep rising to the academic challenge, even when it gets difficult. I fully believe your extraordinary effort also includes improving your self-awareness and learning how you will adapt to life's challenges as you design the life you want to live after college. If you do what the average person does—what our built-in human nature tells us to do—you'll be just like every other average college student. Don't choose to be that average person! Remember your thoughts and actions create your results and are therefore a self-fulfilling prophecy. So manage them wisely.

Allow me to introduce you to your edge, the strategy that will practically ensure that every one of your goals is realized.

The Miracle Equation

Unwavering Faith + Extraordinary Effort = Miracles

It's easier than you think. The secret to maintaining unwavering faith is to recognize that it's a mindset and a *strategy*—it's not concrete. In fact, it's elusive. You can never make *every* grade. No athlete makes *every* shot. You can never win every challenge as a college student. So, you have to program yourself automatically to have the unwavering faith to drive you to keep putting forth the extraordinary effort— regardless of the results.

Remember that the key to putting this equation into practice, to maintaining unwavering faith in the midst of self-doubt, is the Miracle Mantra:

I will _____, no matter what. There is no other option.

Once you set a goal, put that goal into the Miracle Mantra format. Yes, you're going to say your affirmations every morning and maybe every evening, too. But all day, every day, you're going to repeat your Miracle Mantra to yourself. As you're driving or taking the bus to school, while you're on the treadmill, in the shower, in line at the grocery store—in other words, *everywhere you go.*

Your Miracle Mantra will fortify your faith and be the self-talk you need to make just one more try after try.

Bonus Lesson

Remember what I learned from my mentor Dan Casetta on the purpose of goals. You have to become the type of person who *can* achieve the goal. You won't always reach the goal, but you can become someone who maintains unwavering faith and puts forth extraordinary effort regardless of your results. That's how you become the type of person you need to become to achieve extraordinary goals consistently.

And while reaching the goal almost doesn't matter (*almost!*), more often than not, you'll reach your goal. Do the elite athletes win every time? No. But they win most of the time. And you'll win most of the time, too.

You can wake up earlier, do the Life S.A.V.E.R.S. with passion and excitement, get organized, focused, and intentional, and master every challenge like a champ. And yet at the end of the day, if you don't combine unwavering faith with extraordinary effort, you won't reach the levels of success you seek.

The Miracle Equation gives you access to forces outside of anyone's understanding, using an energy that you might call God, the Universe, the Law of Attraction, or even good luck. I don't know *how* it works; I only know *that* it works.

You've read this far—you clearly want success more than almost anything. Commit to following through with every aspect of being a student, including the Miracle Equation. You deserve it, and I want you to have it!

Putting It into Action:

Write out the Miracle Equation and put it where you will see it every day: **Unwavering Faith + Extraordinary Effort = Miracles (UF + EE = M∞)**

What's your number one goal for your journey as a student this year? What goal, if you were to accomplish it, would bring you closest to your ideal academic life?

Write your Miracle Mantra: *I will _____ (insert your goals and daily actions here), no matter what. There is no other option.*

It is more about who you become in the process. You'll expand your self-confidence and, regardless of your results, the very next time you attempt to reach a goal, and every time after that, you'll be the type of person who gives it all they've got.

CLOSING REMARKS

Congratulations! You have done what only a small percentage of people do: read an entire book. If you've come this far, that tells me something about you: You have a thirst for more. You want to become more, do more, contribute more, and earn more.

Right now, you have the unprecedented opportunity to infuse your daily life with the Life S.A.V.E.R.S., upgrade your daily routine, and ultimately upgrade your *life* to a first-class experience beyond your wildest dreams. Before you know it, you will be reaping the astronomical benefits of the habits that top achievers use daily.

Five years from now, your health, happiness, professional life, relationships, and income will be a direct result of one thing: *who you've become.* It's up to you to wake up each day and dedicate time to becoming the best version of yourself. Seize this moment in time, define a vision for your future, and use what you've learned in this book to turn your vision into your reality.

Imagine a time just a few years from now when you come across the journal you started after completing this book. In it, you find the goals you wrote down for yourself—dreams you didn't dare speak out loud at the time. And as you look around, you realize *your dreams now represent the life you are living.*

Right now, you stand at the foot of a mountain you can easily and effortlessly climb. All you need to do is continue waking up each day for your Miracle Morning and use the Life S.A.V.E.R.S. day after day, month after month, year after year, as you continue to take your *self,* your *academics,* and your *success* to levels beyond what you've ever experienced before.

Combine your Miracle Morning with a commitment to master the Areas for Exceptional College Students and use the Miracle Equation to create results that most people only dream of.

This book was written as an expression of what we know will work for you, to take every area of your life to the next level faster than you may currently believe is possible. Miraculous performers weren't born that way—they have simply dedicated their lives to developing themselves and their skills to achieve everything they've ever wanted.

You can become one of them, I promise.

LET TODAY BE THE DAY YOU GIVE UP WHO YOU'VE BEEN FOR WHO YOU CAN BECOME

Every day, think as you wake up, "Today I am fortunate to have woken up, I am alive, I have a precious human life, I am not going to waste it. I am going to use all my energies to develop myself, to expand my heart out to others. I am going to benefit others as much as I can."

—DALAI LAMA

Things do not change. We change.

—HENRY DAVID THOREAU

W here you are is a result of who you were, but where you go from here depends entirely on who you choose to be from this moment forward.

Now is your time. Decide that today is the most important day of your life because it is who you are becoming now—based on the choices that you make and the actions that you take—which will determine who and where you are going to be for the rest of your life.

Don't put off creating and experiencing the life—happiness, health, wealth, success, and love—that you truly want and deserve.

As Kevin Bracy, one of my mentors, always urged, "Don't wait to be great." If you want your life to improve, you have to improve yourself first. You can download the 30-Day Miracle Morning Fast-Start Kit at www.TMMBook.com. Then, with or without an accountability partner, commit to complete your 30-day challenge so that you will immediately begin accessing more of your potential than you ever have before. Imagine … just one month from now, you will be well on your way to transforming every area of your life.

LET'S KEEP HELPING OTHERS

May I ask you a quick favor?

If this book has added value to your life, if you feel like you're better off after reading it, and you see that the Miracle Morning can be a new beginning for you to take any—or every—area of your life to the next level, I'm hoping you'll do something for someone you care about:

Give this book to them or let them borrow your copy. Ask them to read it so that they have the opportunity to transform their life for the better, too. Or, if you're not willing to give up your copy quite yet because you're planning to reread it, you could get them their own copy for no reason other than to say, "Hey, I love and appreciate you, and I want to help you live your best life. Read this."

If you believe as I do that being a great friend (or family member) is about helping your friends and loved ones to become the best versions of themselves, I encourage you to share this book with them.

Together, we are truly elevating the consciousness of humanity, one morning at a time.

Thank you so much.

A SPECIAL INVITATION FROM HAL

Readers and practitioners of *The Miracle Morning* have co-created an extraordinary community consisting of over 200,000 like-minded individuals from around the world who wake up each day with purpose and dedicate time to fulfilling the unlimited potential that is within all of us, while helping others to do the same.

As author of *The Miracle Morning*, I felt I had a responsibility to create an online community where readers could come together to connect, get encouragement, share best practices, support one another, discuss the book, post videos, find accountability partners, and even swap smoothie recipes and exercise routines.

However, I honestly had no idea that The Miracle Morning Community would become one of the most positive, engaged, and supportive online communities in the world—but it has. I'm constantly astounded by the caliber and character of our membership, which presently includes people from over 70 countries and is growing daily.

Just go to **www.MyTMMCommunity.com** and request to join The Miracle Morning Community on Facebook®. You'll immediately be able to connect with 80,000+ people who are already practicing TMM. While you'll find many who are just beginning their Miracle Morning journey, you'll discover even more who have been at it for years and who will happily share advice and guidance to accelerate your success.

I'll be moderating the Community and checking in regularly, so I look forward to seeing you there! If you'd like to reach out to me personally on social media, follow **@HalElrod** on Twitter and **Facebook.com/YoPalHal** on Facebook. Let's connect soon!

ACKNOWLEDGMENTS

I am filled with so much gratitude at this moment, because I know that I could not have created this book without all the experiences that led me here. I fully recognize and understand that I could not have accomplished this dream on my own. It took so many amazing people for this dream to come true! If I thank everyone that comes to mind, this section would be as long as another book!

First, I am grateful to God for all the blessings He has placed in my life. In moments of doubt, You led me to peace, brought me joy, and gave me direction.

Mom, Dad, and George, I love you all so much. Thank you for being there with me every step of the way throughout my life! Thank you for all the discussions and conversations that have created growth in our family. The amount of love and support is incredible. I would not trade it for the world. We are one of a kind, and I am so proud to be a part of this family.

Hal, you are such a huge part of my life story. Thank you for giving an amazing talk at my high school in 2011. Thank you for writing *The Miracle Morning* in 2012. Thank you for working to make The Miracle Morning movement grow until I got the book in my hands. It's such an honor to be able to say that I wrote a book with you. You are such an inspiration to hundreds of thousands of people all over world! Thank you!!

Honorée, it has been such a dream to be able to learn from you and work with you. This book would not be possible without your dedication and compassion. I am grateful for you and your team for all the work you did to make this book the best that it can be. I am grateful for all the lessons you have taught me during this writing journey. I look up to you so much. Thank you for everything!

To my alma mater, Loyola Marymount University: Thank you for giving me four beautiful college years. Without LMU, this book would not have been possible. To everyone in the Frank R. Seaver College of Science and Engineering, thank you for challenging me to become a better student and problem solver. From the labs to studying abroad, I am forever grateful for the education I received and the friendships I made amongst you all. To all the people I worked with and was able to serve as part of the First Year Experience and Resident Housing Association offices, thank you for giving me the opportunities to grow as a leader to serve students. To the ladies of Gryphon Circle Service Organization and Sister Peg: Thank you for leading lives of service and inspiring me daily to be with and for others. To the friends I made at LMU that I consider family (Veronica of M.V., Sarabella, Nadine, Catalina, Taylor, Sarah, Vinny, Lauren, Alex, Steven, Dakota, Nic, Lacey, Katelyn, Genesis, Kimmy, Fiona, Zoe, Kyra, Kendra, Emily, and so many more): Thank you for being such passionate and intelligent individuals. To anyone I have met while at LMU: Thank you for bringing so much joy into my life! LMU Class of 2016, I love you all so much. GO LIONS!

Thank you Akademie für Internationale Bildung for giving me the greatest study abroad experience I could have imagined. You have instilled in me a love for traveling. Because of this program, I was able to expand the vision of what was possible for me in my life. Thank you to Dr. Rainer Zäck, Olivia Schaefer, Stefan Eggers, Hilde Koch, Mira Arbeiter, the amazing staff, and all the professors I had while abroad for making Bonn, Germany feel like home.

Jeff Hoffman, thank you for writing the foreword of this book. As an individual, you inspire me to dream bigger and create real impact in the world. Your success is my miracle. I cannot wait to continue learning from you as you continue to live a life of integrity and service to others. Thank you for expanding the vision of what is possible for me. I am so grateful for you.

To Flintridge Sacred Heart Academy, thank you for giving me a fruitful high school education that allowed me to be accepted into LMU. Sister Celeste and Sister Carolyn, thank you for your leadership and dedication to FSHA and for creating an atmosphere of growth and support. During my time on the Hill, I learned that dreams can come true. Thank you for allowing my cultural history project to make real change in the school curriculum. Thank you to all my teachers and to my classmates in the Class of 2012. I am proud to be a T.O.L.O.G.!

Dan Casetta, you have made a tremendous impact in my life. You have mentored the people I look up to—your leadership has directly had an influence in my life. Thank you for all the time you have dedicated to growing people in Vector Marketing and continuing your leadership. Thank you for being such a great example of what great leadership looks like, and I hope to emulate that in the years ahead.

To my grandmas, aunts, and uncles, thank you all for the constant love and support toward my dreams. You all have never missed a single event in my life, and I am so grateful for each of you! To my grandpas in heaven, thank you for watching over me!

To *all* the cousins, my heart bursts with joy just thinking about you all! You guys have truly been my #1 fans, and I appreciate you all so much. Thank you for all the laughs and being so awesome! We cannot choose family, but I would choose all of you over and over again if I had the choice! Hugs and kisses sent your way!

Arda, thank you for being my best friend. I love you so much. You are always there for me. I am grateful to know that anywhere I go, you'll always be there cheering me on!

To these two communities, The Miracle Morning Community and 1Life Fully Lived Community: Thank you so much for being a constant source of love and support in my life. Daily, I am uplifted by you all and your pursuit toward your dreams! I am so grateful to be a part of such positive communities! You are all a part of my circle of influence, and you push me to be my best!

Thank you to the extraordinary leaders I have met, including but not limited to: Ray Lewis, Jon Vroman, Jon Berghoff, Lindsay and

Mike McCarthy, Brianna Greenspan, Andrea Riggs, Theresa Laurico, Lewis Howes, Tim Rhode, Matt Aitchison, Teri Barton, Rhonda Smith, Matthew Duncan, Jeremy "Brotha" James, Brandy and Lance Salazar, Jeff Kaylor, Reyna Marrufo, Justin and Sara Ledford, and Tuan Nguyen. Thank you for constantly inspiring me to learn more and help others along the path.

Finally, to you, the reader: Thank you all so much for your love and dedication to reading this book! I hope that it has brought you an abundance of hope and knowledge you need to take the next steps in your lives. I am grateful to you, because the steps you take to improve your life right now will not only help you, but will also help everyone around you. Thank you for the impact you will have on the world. Let me know if there is any way I can help you or how I can continue to add value to your life. Be bold, and dream a bigger dream!

ABOUT THE AUTHORS

HAL ELROD is on a mission to *Elevate the Consciousness of Humanity, One Morning at a Time.* As one of the highest rated keynote speakers in the America, creator of one of the fastest growing and most engaged online communities in existence and author of one of the highest rated books in the world, *The Miracle Morning*—which has been translated into 27 languages, has over 2,000 five-star Amazon reviews and is practiced daily by over 500,000 people in 70+ countries—he is doing exactly that.

The seed for Hal's life's work was planted at age twenty, when Hal was found dead at the scene of a horrific car accident. Hit head-on by a drunk driver at seventy miles per hour, he broke eleven bones, died for six minutes, and suffered permanent brain damage. After six days in a coma, he woke to face his unimaginable reality—which included being told by doctors that he would never walk again.

Defying the logic of doctors and proving that all of us can overcome even seemingly insurmountable adversity to achieve anything we set our minds to, Hal went on to not only walk but to run a 52-mile ultramarathon and become a hall of fame business achiever—all before the age of 30.

Then, in November of 2016, Hal nearly died again. With his kidneys, lungs, and heart of the verge of failing, he was diagnosed with a very rare, very aggressive form of leukemia and given a 30% chance of living. After enduring the most difficult year of his life, Hal is now cancer-free and furthering his mission as the Executive Producer of *The Miracle Morning Movie.*

Most importantly, Hal is beyond grateful to be sharing his life with the woman of his dreams, Ursula Elrod, and their two children in Austin, Texas.

For more information on Hal's keynote speaking, live events, books, the movie and more, visit www.HalElrod.com.

NATALIE JANJI is a graduate of Loyola Marymount University and has a bachelor's degree in chemistry. After reading *The Miracle Morning* book, she became aware of her growing passion to help college students live to their full potential. Natalie is currently a speaker, coach, and author ready to set the world on fire (figuratively). You can find out more about her at NatalieJanji.com.

HONORÉE CORDER is the author of dozens of books, including *You Must Write a Book, The Prosperous Writers* book series, *Like a Boss* book series, *Vision to Reality, Business Dating, The Successful Single Mom* book series, *If Divorce is a Game, These are the Rules,* and *The Divorced Phoenix.* She is also Hal Elrod's business partner in *The Miracle Morning* book series. Honorée coaches business professionals, writers, and aspiring non-fiction authors who want to publish their books to bestseller status, create a platform, and develop multiple streams of income. She also does all sorts of other magical things, and her badassery is legendary. You can find out more at HonoreeCorder.com.

THE MIRACLE MORNING SERIES

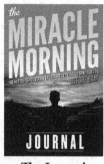

The Journal

for Salespeople

for Real Estate Agents

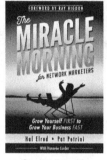

for Network Marketers

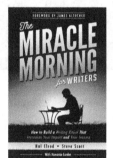

for Writers

for Entrepreneurs

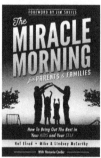

for Parents & Families

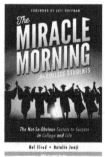

for College Students

COMPANION GUIDES & WORKBOOKS

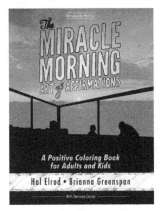

Art of Affirmations

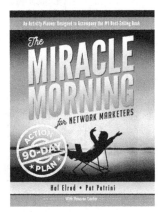

**for Network Marketers
90-Day Action Plan**

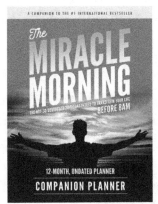

Companion Planner

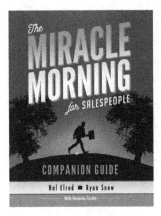

**for Salespeople
Companion Guide**

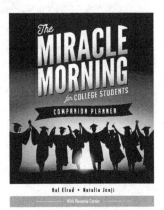

**for College Students
Companion Planner**

HAL ELROD & JON BERGHOFF

PRESENT...

BEST YEAR EVER BLUEPRINT

ONE WEEKEND CAN CHANGE YOUR LIFE.
JOIN US FOR THIS ONCE-IN-A-LIFETIME EXPERIENCE.

www.BestYearEverLive.com

Most personal development events cause "information overload" and often leave attendees feeling more overwhelmed than when they arrived. You end up with pages and pages of notes, then you go home and have to figure out how and when to implement everything you've learned.

Co-hosted by experiential trainer, Jon Berghoff, the **Best Year Ever Blueprint LIVE** event won't just teach you how to change your life, you'll actually starting taking steps to *change your life while you're still at the event*.

"I truly had a life changing weekend during BYEB2015. I feel as if my mind has hit a 'reset' button. Reading The Miracle Morning and coming to the live event has been a gift, and the best investment in myself I've ever made. I am excited to take this momentum and create my level 10 life next year!"

Ericka Staples

seeQus
MARKETING TECHNOLOGIES

BULLETPROOF.
POWER MIND AND BODY

Learn more about the Best Year Ever event online at
WWW.BESTYEAREVERLIVE.COM

Made in the USA
Coppell, TX
13 May 2020

25522606R00134